THE NATION AT WAR

Arthur Stein teaches
in the political science department
at the University of California,
Los Angeles.

The Nation at War

ARTHUR A. STEIN

War is father of all—HERACLITUS

The Johns Hopkins University Press

Baltimore and London

Printed in the United States of America

The Johns Hopkins University Press, Baltimore,
Maryland 21218

The Johns Hopkins Press Ltd., London

Library of Congress Cataloging in Publication Data

Stein, Arthur A.
  The Nation at war.

  Bibliography: pp. 125–41
  Includes index.
  1. War and society. 2. Politics and war.
3. War—Economic aspects—United States. I. Title.
HM36.5.S73   303.6′6   80-7994
ISBN 0-8018-2441-9

For My Mother
and in Memory of My Father
Mila Stein and Joseph Stein (ז׳ל)

CONTENTS

FIGURES

TABLES

ix / Contents

ACKNOWLEDGMENTS

I HAVE accumulated many intellectual debts in writing this book, and it is a pleasure to acknowledge them here, although thanks are not really enough.

I will always be grateful to two teachers who introduced me to the study of international politics. Walter LaFeber fostered in me a love of diplomatic history and a commitment to teaching. Richard Rosecrance linked history with social science and introduced me to international relations theory. They remain personal as well as academic models.

I am also grateful to Bruce Russett, H. Bradford Westerfield, and Raymond Duvall, who continued my education in international politics and encouraged me throughout the ordeal of graduate training. I am especially thankful for Bruce Russett's expert guidance throughout.

All of them, at one time or another, provided criticism and advice on all or parts of various incarnations of this work. Early on I was also helped by Christopher Achen, Paul Berman, and Harris Miller. More recently, colleagues and friends, Robert Jervis and Stephen D. Krasner, provided useful advice and criticism.

In addition to intellectual debts, I would have accumulated larger economic ones were it not for the financial assistance that came from many quarters. I would like to acknowledge the generosity of Yale University, the International Studies Association, the University Consortium for World Order Studies, the Jewish Community Federation of Cleveland for the Morris Abrams Award in International Relations, and the Academic Senate of the University of California, Los Angeles. These institutions and individuals are absolved from any responsibility for what follows.

xi

I would also like to thank Henry Y. K. Tom of the Johns Hopkins University Press for his guidance, and Mary Lou Kenney and C. S. Steinger for prompt and thoughtful editing.

The figures for this book were drawn by Noël L. Diaz, UCLA cartographer. His impeccable artwork truly allows figures to meet the interocular test of significance.

My thanks also to Lynn Panza, Doreen Bodin, and Lyndell Betzner for typing the original manuscript.

This work is dedicated to my parents, whose work it really is. It was their faith and sacrifice that made it possible. Their efforts are worthy of a masterpiece; I offer this instead. No thanks will ever do.

My wife, Amy, shared the pangs of this birth. She provided the time, space, support, and assistance that I needed. This is in many ways her handiwork, for she made it literate. Only now can I thank her for her periodic attempts to divert my attention to what is really important.

THE NATION AT WAR

INTRODUCTION: WAR, THE STATE, AND SOCIETY

WAR IS the raison d'être of the state, yet we know little about its impact on state and society. It is not as if we neglect the study of war altogether; we understand a great deal about its origins, the ways in which it is fought, and how it changes politics between nations. Yet for all we know about peace treaties and battlefields, we remain too little aware of the home-front. For all our interest in the desired outcomes and unintended consequences of many government programs, war remains the least evaluated of public policies.[1] This book is about the domestic ramifications of war.

We do not fail to study war's effects because wars are rare. Only 227 of the 3,364 years from 1496 B.C.E. to 1868 C.E. were unmarked by a war somewhere in the world.[2] Only 24 of the 150 years between 1816 and 1965 were warless,[3] and over 110 million people have lost their lives in war during the twentieth century alone.[4] Nor is it the case that we find war's consequences trivial. Recognizing that wars are an important agent of political, economic, and social change, scholars often use them to mark major turning points in human history, to separate one historical period from another.

Nonetheless, it is hard to find recent studies of the effects of war. There was greater interest in war's consequences earlier in the century, however, particularly during and after World War I. The Carnegie Endowment for International Peace, for example, published a 150-volume series on *The Economic and Social History of the World War,* much of which was devoted to the

1

effects of the "Great War" on society, politics, and economics in the involved nations.[5]

Yet World War I was not "the war to end all wars," and World War II also sparked interest in the ramifications of war. Scholars were tremendously concerned with assessing the war's vast transformations of American society, and the Social Science Research Council established a Committee on War Studies to do just that. By 1948, however, the committee was disbanded, with most of its work left uncompleted or unpublished.[6]

There is a problem in that these earlier works predate the transformation of the study of politics into a social science built on theory and comparative assessment. Most are descriptions of the effects of a given war on a particular facet of one nation's domestic life. Even recently, there have been few attempts to subsume discrete manifestations of change into larger concepts, or to compare the effects of war and make general statements about them.

The spirit of the times affects scholars, and although they certainly acknowledge the effects of World War II, those very consequences changed their study of war. It was during the postwar period that the study of "politics" became the study of "political science," but at the same time, international relations specialists abandoned their investigations of war's consequences and turned instead to studying war causation, crisis, and arms races. For most, "once a war happens it ceases to be interesting."[7] The advent of the Cold War and the nuclear age brought about a scholarly reorientation, and the focus of work shifted to the prevention of the next war, one many feared would be the world's last. Students of war took on the task of helping to avoid it, and thus turned to an investigation of its causes. If they understood why wars began, then maybe international relations specialists could practice a kind of preventive medicine. As it became clear that the existence of nuclear weapons did not put an end to confrontations between nations, they turned their attention to the problems of crisis and crisis management, to the requirements of maintaining peace when war most threatened. Yet we now know that crises have not, after all, become our only international problems; war can still occur in a nuclear age. The superpowers have not been able to prevent conventional wars between nonnuclear powers, nor to avoid their own involvement in them. Thus, to study war's consequences remains important and timely.

The study of war's ramifications has more than intrinsic scholarly interest, however; it can also be of concrete and immediate utility to political leaders. Those who make the decisions to involve or to risk involving their nations in war must assess probable outcomes and consequences in doing so. Policymakers hoping to make more rational cost-benefit calculations about whether or not to go to war have little scholarly guidance because of the paucity of work in this field. They cannot properly assess the unintended effects that their actions might induce, and are typically aware only of the costs that would be exacted if they do not go to war while imagining the benefits of a successful military solution to an immediate problem. Yet they should be aware of all possible ramifications, desired and undesired, and this requires an understanding of war's domestic effects. Quite simply, policymakers should treat the decision to go to war as they would the decision to implement any other program and ask themselves two simple questions: Will the policy accomplish those goals for which it is intended? Is it likely to have any unanticipated or unintended costs that might make it a poor means to the goal or that might require attention if the decision is made to go to war anyway and suffer the undesired consequences? Knowing about war's side effects may prevent leaders from waging war; if not, it can certainly assist them in minimizing or preparing for its undesired impact on domestic life.

This book is a two-part study of war's domestic consequences. The first develops the links between war and domestic cohesion, concentration, and inequality. All three are critical features of the nation-state. Social unity, for example, is at the very heart of national existence; without it, there can be no society and no nation. Concentration is no less a defining characteristic than cohesion, however. In its political manifestation, concentration defines the role of the state vis-à-vis the society and the economy, describing the extent to which political power is centralized in one place and in few hands. Concentration refers not only to the size and scope of the state, however, but to the economy as well, to the way in which a society is organized for production. Both wartime mobilization and the state can affect the production process, as they can affect inequality, a characteristic of both economy and society. The final feature of domestic life discussed here, inequality, refers to the uneven extraction and distribution of goods from and to a nation's people; it is, therefore, a critical political issue.

Thus, this book focuses on the bases of domestic politics that are central concerns of political science. By affecting domestic cohesion, war may touch the very heart of a nation. It may also alter the relationships between state, society, and economy. If so, we should know how.

When a nation goes to war, all of its people are necessarily involved. It is a societal undertaking that affects everyone and of which all are aware. Some social scientists argue that it knits society together, that what they variously call unity, togetherness, solidarity, and cohesion increases in wartime. Many fondly recall the American involvement in World War II as an experience that united people in a common endeavor. Some even argue that war can create national solidarity where none previously existed. Indeed, the Russian Minister of the Interior remarked in 1904 that "what this country needs is a short victorious war to stem the tide of revolution."[8]

Others believe, however, that war can tear a society apart and point to the

American involvement in Vietnam as having done just that. At the extreme, the Russian experiences in 1905 and 1917 suggest that war can literally rend the national fabric and bring civil war or revolution, not exactly what the Interior Minister had in mind. The arguments on both sides seem plausible, but we do not know which is correct. The answer may be that war can serve either to increase or decrease domestic cohesion, depending on the circumstances.

If political leaders accept the notion that external conflict increases national unity, they may start wars and create international incidents in order to solidify their political positions and erase domestic division.[9] If so, elite insecurity and domestic fragmentation are one root of war and imperialism. If there have indeed been wars begun for domestic reasons, then it is ironic that we do not know if such wars serve to strengthen the elite's hand, or if the opposite is perhaps true: that starting war for domestic political purposes actually damages their standing, undercutting their already weakened position.

Even if national leaders do not start wars because of domestic concerns, they should still assess the domestic ramifications of foreign policy on their positions, programs, and indeed, their ability to sustain the war effort. This is especially the case in the modern era of "total war," in which the homefront is essential to military victory. For any one of a number of reasons, then, this study's conclusions about war's impact on domestic cohesion is of interest to many audiences, both leaders and followers.

War's direct effects on society are accompanied by economic and political consequences as well. Mobilizing for war may well necessitate changes in the way a society is organized for production and in the role of government, both as mobilizing agent and as one element of the productive process. It is government that wages war and organizes society for doing so, and war and the state thus have a strong symbiotic relationship. As Charles Tilly puts it, "war made the state and the state makes war."[10] Indeed, the foremost function of the state is to provide collective security, and many argue that individuals create governments to protect themselves, accepting coercion and permitting the state to extract resources in return for the provision of this collective good. Its ability to wage war thus provides the state with purpose and legitimacy. In this way, war makes the state.

The development of the state, which grows as it extracts more resources from the society during the course of mobilization, is typically accompanied by an increase in the scope of governmental responsibility. War may well affect the balance between central and local governments, leading to greater political centralization or concentration. Similarly, wartime mobilization can effect changes in the way the society and the economy are organized for the war effort and for the production and provision of critical goods and services.

Finally, this book investigates the relationship between war, the state, and societal inequality. The state can affect inequality by the particular means of extraction it chooses for wartime mobilization, and it is not immediately obvious whether wartime extraction is more or less equitable than peacetime extraction. The state also distributes goods and services and affects inequality in this way. Especially in the twentieth century, states have become increasingly committed both to overseeing the working of the private marketplace and to providing services directly in the form of social welfare expenditures. We do not know, however, if welfare expenditures increase or decrease in wartime, if military expenditures squeeze out social service expenditures, or if perhaps the government has both increased resources and increased interest in the welfare of its citizenry during wartime—if, in other words, war increases or decreases domestic inequality.

The trauma of war lingers in other societies in a way that it has not in the United States, save, of course, for the South in the late nineteenth century. Unlike Europeans, Americans do not have an ingrained sense of the ramifications of war. Americans tend to put their wars behind them; they are not continually confronted with the ravages of battle after peace has been restored. The natural defenses of the United States have often assured its security and insulation, and Americans have suffered great destruction only in civil wars. Europe has been a battlefield, whereas the United States has escaped from conflict relatively unscathed during the last 100 years. To Americans, war is something they go off to fight and come home to forget—it does not come to them.

For this reason, an analysis of war's effects on the United States provides an excellent test case for the propositions developed in the first part of this book. The costs of war borne by the United States have been slight compared to those borne by the other major powers during the twentieth century. The nation suffered little physical destruction, was never occupied, and suffered no outright military defeat. To find that war has strongly affected twentieth-century American life would be especially compelling, therefore, and would eliminate the possibility that devastation and conquest alone effect changes in domestic life. In addition, the four American wars of the twentieth century have varied in magnitude, severity, and importance, and that too allows for careful comparison and control.

This book differs from much recent scholarship not only in its specific subject, the ramifications of war, but in that it investigates consequences at all. Scholarship is arbitrarily divided into disciplines and subfields that bring together students of like approaches to related problems. Typically, the social sciences, and to a lesser extent history, have been devoted to uncovering causes; scholars in international relations, for example, typically study the causes of war. When they look outside political science for inspiration and ideas, they go to those disciplines and subfields that are devoted to the investigation of similar phenomena such as sociological studies of the roots of urban conflict.

In approaching the problem of war from the other direction, this book contributes to those fields that study the causes of what are here treated as effects. Thus, it borrows from and contributes to the public finance literature, which investigates the determinants of government expenditures, to the sociological literatures on the causes of cohesion and stratification, to the economics literature on income inequality, to historical studies of change in twentieth-century America, and to the multidisciplinary literature on the origins of the state and its development. I hope it will be of interest to scholars in a variety of disciplines.

More importantly, however, this book is a step in the evaluation of war as public policy. It specifically assesses consequences that are usually unintended and often unanticipated. It should assist those charged with mobilizing a nation for war in dealing with problems that arise as by-products. Although incorporating these domestic effects of war into policy-makers' original calculations as costs and benefits will not spell an end to war, it will, I hope, make their decisions more intelligent and more rational.

PART I

THE DOMESTIC EFFECTS
OF WAR

1

THREAT, MOBILIZATION, AND COHESION

WAR BRINGS the members of society together. The assumption is a common one. Wars, despite their horrors, are often remembered nostalgically, as times when everyone pitched in, gladly did without, and worked together to meet the challenge of the crisis. An extension of this basic argument is that war not only increases national solidarity but can actually create it. Thus, scholars often suggest that Bismarck used the Austro-Prussian War of 1866 and the Franco-Prussian War of 1870 to forge a united German nation.[1]

At the same time, many others believe that war is a cause of social disintegration, that nations at war tend to fragment and become internally discordant. The American experience in Vietnam is typically portrayed in this fashion, as is turn-of-the-century Russia.[2] There, an abortive revolution began during the Russo-Japanese War of 1905, and a successful one overthrew the Tsarist government during World War I.

Despite their differences, the proponents of these two arguments share a common assumption, that war somehow affects, either positively or negatively, the feelings that individuals hold for their nation and for each other, an aspect of society variously termed unity, togetherness, cohesiveness, and solidarity. Historians and political scientists have generally assumed the existence of such a relationship without further question, and have treated war as a cause of both increased and decreased social solidarity. Sociologists, anthropologists, and psychologists, on the other hand, have dealt more analytically with the general relationship between conflict and cohesion. More

9

important, they provide a definition of cohesion that is useful, that of the attraction of group members for one another or the probability of individuals remaining in the group.[3]

The general proposition common to these disciplines is that a group's involvement in an external conflict increases its internal cohesion. This hypothesis originated in sociology, where it is assumed to carry the highest degree of confirmation. It appears in propositional inventories[4] and has been referred to as a "general law"[5] and a "ubiquitous principle."[6] Interestingly enough, there are few statements of the counter-hypothesis,[7] and the wholehearted acceptance of the proposition's veracity has meant that some of the intervening variables or necessary preconditions outlined by the thesis's developers have been forgotten by their successors. Also, sociologists have done relatively little empirical work designed to validate or falsify the proposition. It appears that plausibility and multiple references carry their own confirmation, even without proper testing. Social psychologists have tested the hypothesis, but most of the sociologists who so readily accept the proposition are unaware of these empirical studies. Similarly, the social psychologists are generally oblivious to the sociologists' theoretical work.

Analysis of the psychologists' situational and experimental studies suggests that external conflict does increase internal group cohesion, but only under certain circumstances.[8] A number of intervening variables pertaining to the nature of the group and the conflict are necessary for the relationship to hold. These are outlined in table 1-1.

Of these, the most important is threat. It is critical that the individual members of a group all believe that the external conflict constitutes a threat to the existence of the collectivity. All of the other conditions are ancillary. First, the group must have existed prior to the onset of threat. Second, its members must believe that the threat affects the entire collectivity; if only a subset of individuals is threatened, overall group cohesion may not increase.[9] All must be affected indiscriminately; the danger and suffering must become public phenomena and, in a sense, shared equally. Third, all must believe the threat to be external, as emanating from a source outside the group. The members of the collectivity cannot themselves be associated with it. In addition, the group must be seen as being able to deal with the external threat. Individuals become more attracted to the group when they believe mutual effort is central to goal attainment, when they believe a group solution to the external threat is possible and an individual response is not. Finally, the individual must not be able to escape the threat; only cooperative behavior can reduce or eliminate it and thus protect the single member.

Often, social scientists suggest that war is the prototypical example of an external conflict that leads to increased internal cohesion. The reason is that if a war involves a threat to the nation then the other necessary conditions are

TABLE 1-1
Requisites for External Conflict to Increase Internal Group Cohesion

---

A. Nature of the External Conflict
    1. Involves a threat
    2. Source of threat external
    3. Threat to entire group
    4. Threat amenable to cooperative solution
    5. All of the above must be perceived by all the individuals comprising the group
B. Nature of the Group
    1. Existence must predate the occurrence of the external conflict

---

all generally present: the nation has existed as an entity prior to the war,[10] and the entire nation is externally threatened.[11] Thus, only cooperative solutions are possible, and there is generally popular expectation of success.[12]

Threat is the only intervening variable which does not always accompany international wars. A victorious aggressor nation is rarely threatened by the wars it initiates.[13] Clearly, threat is a variable.[14] A nation's people clearly perceive threat when their country is directly attacked and its physical and territorial integrity is at stake. When a war does involve a threat to the nation, it can be assumed that the other conditions also apply. Thus, it would be expected that the threatened nation would experience an increase in domestic cohesion.

> H1: The involvement of a nation in an international war will lead to an increase in its internal cohesion if its people believe both that the war constitutes an external threat to the nation's survival and that cooperative effort will bring ultimate success.

This formulation is inadequate, however, in that it fails to recognize the role of time. This problem follows from a similar weakness in the studies on which the proposition is based, most of which are atemporal. Typically, social psychologists test the hypothesis by exposing a group to a threatening situation and taking a single observation immediately afterwards. This procedure can only ascertain changes in group cohesion that immediately follow the group's exposure to an external threat. Yet real-world conflicts are often protracted, and it is likely that their course also effects changes in internal cohesion.[15] More importantly, the process by which a group engages in conflict may itself effect such changes.

When a nation goes to war, it must utilize a variety of resources in its struggle. This internal national undertaking is generally referred to as mobilization. Here, mobilization is defined as a process by which national elites rapidly gain control of resources for the purpose of waging war. Although mobilization can, of course, be undertaken for other reasons, the focus here is solely on mobilization for war.

National leaders are continually involved in extracting resources from the populace and then expending them in a variety of ways. National governments almost universally levy taxes and spend that revenue for numerous goods and services. Cash may well be the most important resource that governments extract, a means by which they can purchase and thus control a variety of additional resources. There are other ways, however, in which leaders can gain control of resources. Governments can command the donation of goods and services other than cash, with or without remuneration. These resources are typically used to provide the members of the society with a variety of goods and services. In wartime, however, the extraction increases, as additional resources are required for the express purpose of waging war. Thus, wartime mobilization can be a simple extension of peacetime extraction, as more is taken from the population by familiar means for special purposes. Often, however, the extraction process itself changes, as does the kind of goods extracted. Requisition may become more common, for example, and conscription may be instituted in order to extract the resource of human labor.

Thus, there are two aspects of wartime mobilization that differentiate it from normal governmental extraction. The first is that the process entails the extraction of resources not ordinarily controlled by government. The second unique characteristic of wartime mobilization is that its purpose, and thus the nature of its benefits to the individual members of society, is clearly specified. This latter feature is particularly important because it allows the citizens of the warring nation to calculate the costs and benefits of their involvement in the conflict more directly than those of typical governmental operations.

Generally, public transactions between individuals and governments involve no direct link between costs and benefits. Although an individual can often calculate quite precisely the costs and benefits of a freely chosen private transaction, the often coercive public exchange remains a mystery. The most obvious reason for this is that governments provide benefits without direct payment on the part of the individual. Then too, governments may provide a good or service to one segment of a society at another's expense. Taxpayers know only vaguely how and in what proportion their taxes are spent. Many government actions are secret, semisecret, or public but not highly visible. No citizen, not even a chief executive, has complete information about the scope and costs of governmental action. In wartime, however, it is clearly apparent that the extra increment of extraction is spent on the war effort. The uses to which mobilized resources are put are often readily apparent. Thus, it is easier for individuals to calculate the utility to them of various governmental actions. Parents whose children are sent into battle, for example, can make a clear connection between the cost they bear and the benefit they receive.

Such calculations are simplified during wartime not only because benefits become more obvious, but because the taxes of wartime mobilization (meaning all of the resources extracted for war purposes) are also more clearly visible than are those in peacetime. It is axiomatic that government costs are always highly apparent, especially relative to benefits. Similarly, individuals are generally more aware of what they pay than of what they receive. Yet governments do attempt to mask the burden, often employing indirect taxes in order to avoid citizen reprisals. In time of war, however, the extraction process becomes even more apparent, and the situation in which individuals find taxes to be more "real" than benefits becomes exacerbated. Often, direct taxes increase drastically in relation to indirect ones.

Again, wartime allows individuals to calculate the costs and benefits of public policy more readily. War is a highly visible form of governmental policy, and it brings the role of the government into stark relief. Strategy and tactics may remain secret, but the actual involvement in conflict and its goals cannot usually be hidden. At the same time, the mobilization process is highly visible, and individuals are likely to have an easier time than usual in comparing what they pay with what they receive.[16]

One factor that complicates such cost-benefit analyses is the nature of the good that the government provides, whether it is a private or a public (collective) one. Private goods are those that the members of society consume as individuals, even if the goods are provided by the public sector. A public good, on the other hand, is one that is commonly enjoyed "in the sense that each individual's consumption of such a good leads to no subtraction from any other individual's consumption of that good."[17] Clearly, therefore, it is to the individual's advantage to minimize his or her contribution to the provision of such goods, since the good's consumption cannot be denied to any single individual or even to any group of persons that is a subset of the entire society. Either everybody gets it, or nobody does. The difficulty that then arises is known as the "free rider" problem. In wartime, this problem can be especially troubling because the provision of national defense is unambiguously a collective good. All members of a nation benefit from the provision of defense or the waging of war in the face of threat. This good cannot be provided to some without being provided to all. The problem is that the good's provision is accompanied by the process of extraction, and the individual's incentive is to provide as little as possible in return for the good received.

... the benefits of national defense are collective in nature; that is, if they exist for one man, all men enjoy them [women too]. This fact makes quid pro quo transactions impossible, because once the benefit exists, enjoyment of it cannot be denied to those citizens who have not paid for it. For this reason, voluntary payment cannot be used to finance collective benefits. Since each citizen benefits whether or not he has paid, he maximizes his income by dodging his share of the cost. But everyone has this cost-minimizing attitude; so if voluntary payment is relied upon, no one pays. Consequently the resources necessary to provide the collective good are not provided and no one receives any benefits. To avoid this outcome, individuals agree to coerce each other into payment through a collective agency like the government.[18]

Quite simply, the wartime mobilization process is a form of taxation for the provision of a collective good in a context where individuals can decide relatively easily whether this highly visible governmental policy is a wise one.[19] Whatever they decide, however, individuals who are called upon to make sacrifices when the nation is threatened are likely to want to minimize their personal contribution even if they believe that there is a legitimate threat and recognize the need for national action. In other words, even if they believe that the war is necessary and that the government is doing a good job of waging it, they are likely to resent the taxes they must pay to provide this legitimate and worthwhile goal.[20]

Thus, the greater the level of mobilization, the greater the probability that no single individual will escape bearing some cost and sacrifice and the greater the amount of the burden that any single individual is asked to bear. Thus, the greater the amount or level of the mobilization effort, the greater the number of individuals who are likely to feel resentment, and the greater the amount of resentment that any single individual is likely to feel. In other words, the greater the degree of mobilization, the less the degree of overall social cohesion. If more individuals are resentful, and if the amount of that resentment on the part of any member of society is greater, then cohesion will decrease as a direct function of the process of extraction.[21]

This conclusion is striking, for it posits that the mobilization process undertaken in order to wage the war serves to decrease the level of domestic cohesion independently of those aspects of conflict that tend to increase the affiliative tendencies of the members of a society. This is not to say that individuals will not support a war effort, for they generally do. In the face of threat, national security is a paramount priority. But it is precisely because this good is collective that individuals resent the ever greater sacrifices that they are called upon to make, even if they very much want the benefits they receive in return.[22]

> H2: Domestic cohesion decreases as a function of increases in the level of wartime mobilization.

The links between war and cohesion, and mobilization and cohesion, are derived separately here, and it is assumed that they are independent of one another. It is expected that an immediate increase in cohesion will follow the onset of any conflict that manifests the requisite characteristics outlined above. During the *course* of the war, however, group cohesion will decrease as a function of the level of mobilization. During the early stages of a war, the behavioral manifestations of individual attraction to the group would be very much in evidence. Individuals might be expected to swamp induction centers and make voluntary contributions to government agencies not yet equipped to handle them. As time passes, however, voluntarism would be likely to wane, and attempts to circumvent governmental wartime regulations to increase.

When the requisite characteristics are not present, an immediate increase in cohesion is not expected to follow the onset of belligerencies. When threat is not present, mobilization effects an immediate decrease in the level of cohesion. Further, comparable levels of mobilization are likely to affect cohesion differently in wars where threat does and does not exist. In the latter case, the overall decrease in cohesion is expected to be greater. In other words, the marginal decrease in cohesion per unit of mobilization is likely to be greater in the absence of threat.

The model developed in this chapter includes two independent hypotheses. First, that the involvement of a nation in an international war leads to an increase in its internal cohesion if its people believe both that the war constitutes an external threat to the nation and that cooperative effort will lead to ultimate success. Second, it is hypothesized that domestic cohesion decreases as a function of increases in the level of the mobilization undertaken to wage that war.[23] This proposition runs counter both to intuition and longstanding general wisdom, for it has long been assumed that one of the major effects of war is to draw the people of each warring nation together: "There is one thing you have in war that you do not have in peace. You have unification, compelled by a very threatening danger. In other words, Franklin's old saying, 'If we don't hang together, we'll hang separately,' applies more definitely in war than it does in peace."[24] It is not claimed here that threat does not have this effect. It is argued, however, that wartime mobilization serves to decrease the degree of domestic cohesion in the long run, despite the fact that threat tends to increase the affiliative tendencies of the members of the society.

2

THE CONCENTRATION
OF POWER AND
PRODUCTION

MOBILIZING FOR war is a complicated process, one that often entails necessary changes in the organization of production and consumption. This chapter is a discussion of how war affects three critical facets of the productive process: government, industry, and labor.

The state is at the heart of wartime mobilization, for only the state can wage war. Government becomes the coordinating agent that decides which resources to extract and how to apply them to the war effort. It is not surprising, therefore, that war highlights the role of government in the organization of national production.

The factors of production are ubiquitously given as labor, land, and capital, but just as important is the technical, managerial, and organizational expertise that determines how the other three factors are utilized. In other words, the organizational dimension represents an additional factor in the production process. Government is one such organizing institution and is instrumental in maintaining harmony among the various individual interests that come into conflict in any society.

Especially in modern societies, governments often enter the marketplace directly in order to control economic exchanges. They may effect changes in the economy in a variety of ways for a variety of purposes; their goals may range from controlling demand to allocating supplies. Even when a government does not have a specific economic purpose or does not attempt con-

16

sciously to affect the workings of the marketplace or does not even unconsciously intervene in the economy by either direct or indirect means, its policies affect the costs of production.

Waging war is a special type of public policy and can involve an increase in the scope of government activity. Since wartime mobilization refers to the process by which the political elite rapidly gains control of resources and uses them for waging war, the most immediate result of such mobilization is the growth of the central government. If the mobilization is large, then the central state takes over responsibilities and activities normally in the purview of local governments; it can even take on entirely new roles. In other words, a large wartime mobilization can lead to an increase in governmental centralization or concentration, the extent to which the decision-making powers exercised by government officials are confined both to one place and to a small number of individuals. A decentralized government, on the other hand, is one composed of widely dispersed centers of decision-making authority and in which a large number of officials autonomously exercise that authority.

Wartime mobilization engenders political concentration because wars are not run out of local field offices. Unlike education policy, it is not possible for each locality to establish its own war policies, even when it might like to. The Confederate states during the American Civil War provide a paradoxical example of this process of political centralization.[1] The Southern states had seceded from the Union over the issue of slavery and their desire to maintain the plantation system of agriculture. During this long-standing regional dispute, the South had adopted a political philosophy that justified their position; long before the onset of war, they developed the doctrine of states' rights, which asserted that the rights of the individual states took precedence over the authority of the federal government. Ironically, the war of 1861–65 was fought by a ''nation'' that could not in practice recognize the doctrine it propounded. One consequence of the Confederacy's mobilization for war was the concentration of authority, including that over normal production, in one central Southern government.

Wars are fought by national governments because they must be. Thus, unless it is possible to wage war using only preexisting resources, mobilization becomes necessary and leads to an increase in the power of the central government at the expense of local authorities. This occurs not only because the national government wages the war, which becomes the society's foremost public policy, but because the central government's concerns expand to include any other policy, at any level of government, that may affect its ability to wage war. Thus, the increase in political concentration flows from the basic requisites of military organization, including the need for a highly structured hierarchical organization.[2]

Education policy in the United States in the 1940s and 1950s provides another illustration of the federal assumption of local powers given the demands of war. The intimate relationship between American universities and the federal government was forged during World War II, when the central government required skills and research facilities that only the schools could provide.[3] It was during this period that the universities became dependent on government resources for their continued existence. Secondary education, which has always been the responsibility of local officials, was similarly affected. Although Congress had regularly defeated legislation to provide federal aid to education even as late as the middle 1950s, the Soviet launching of Sputnik suggested to many Americans that the United States was on the wrong side not only of a "missile gap" but of an "education gap." Thus, Congress funded the first federal aid-to-education program in 1958 as part of the National Defense Education Act: "History will smile sardonically at the spectacle of this country's getting interested . . . in education only because of the technical achievements of Russia, and then being able to act as a nation only by assimilating education to the cold war and calling an education bill a defense bill."[4]

Any mobilization large enough to increase governmental concentration can also affect the degree of concentration of the other factors of production as well. When the demand generated by the mobilization process exceeds the society's productive capacity, it necessitates changes in the structure of production in order to meet the requirements of wartime mobilizaton. Some of the resources that are mobilized in war are the goods that societies produce. The most obvious of these is military equipment, be it tanks and planes or food and clothing for soldiers. The governmental demand for these goods effects either an increase in production or a transfer of production facilities from the creation of one good to another, from cars to tanks, for example. The greater the level of mobilization, the more that is required. Any initial demand for increased output can be met if there is a slack in already existing production. Thus, if a nation's factories produce at only 50 percent of capacity at war's outset, then increased demand can be met by production at closer to full capacity.

War can, however, require changes in the production structure of a society. Such changes may be required by the demand for new goods, those not ordinarily produced in peacetime. They may also be necessitated by the need to produce beyond full capacity, and such change is often much harder to achieve. In either case, changes in production structures, whether to increase the output of "old" goods or start making "new" ones, require increased efficiency.

To produce more from the same base requires that more be squeezed from the same amount of resources that are normally utilized in the production process. This is typically accomplished through economies of scale, a term that usually refers to the lower cost per unit of output that is realized through higher levels of production, typically achieved by using very large production facilities. Economies of scale need not be just such pecuniary economies, however. There are, for example, real economies that result from a reduction in the physical quantity of resources needed to produce a unit of output; these are, of course, translated into monetary savings. Since large-scale operation is the most accepted way to achieve efficiency, the result is most typically an increase in industrial concentration. Thus, wartime mobilization, once it demands production beyond full capacity or requires the production of ''new'' goods, leads to a greater concentration of production facilities. (Concentration is the ratio of the total amount of a society's production to the number of producing firms. Production is more concentrated if a society's entire output comes from only two firms rather than ten. A similar measure of concentration, one that focuses on the ''top'' of the distribution, is the proportion of total goods produced by some chosen number of a society's largest firms. Thus, a society in which five firms produce 20 percent of its goods is more concentrated than one in which those top five firms produce only 10 percent.)

The process of mobilization also involves the extraction of a wider variety of resources than the goods produced by the society. Some of these resources are themselves factors of production. When governments draft individuals into the army, for example, they gain control of a resource ordinarily used in the peacetime production process, for inductees are taken from a society's private labor pool. It may be possible in a short or minor conflict for a government to draft only the unemployed. But the military often needs skilled workers (those less likely to be out of work), and once mobilization exceeds a certain level, it becomes necessary to draft employed laborers in any case. One result is that the private sector must find replacement labor in order to meet the increased production demands of wartime. One typical solution is migration from the rural sector of a society (which often supports those who would otherwise be jobless by the underemployment of labor) into the cities. In other words, wartime mobilization can induce a migration that increases the concentration of a nation's population. (A low degree of population concentration is manifested by an even distribution of people across the land, the typical pattern of a predominantly agricultural nation. More industrially developed nations, on the other hand, tend to have more concentrated labor forces, with most workers clustered in one or more centralized manufacturing centers.)

Chapter 1 argues that the onset of war has a potentially immediate and independent effect on domestic cohesion because of the impact of the perceived existence of threat. No such linkage is expected in the case of concentration, however. There is simply no reason to expect that involvement in an external conflict in itself effects any changes in the way in which society is organized for productive purposes. Wars do, of course, affect the patterns of international trade and investment, causing changes that might well reverberate through a national production scheme by affecting demand (gain or loss of exports) and supply (gain or loss of imports). Nonetheless, involvement in war does not in itself cause changes in the degree of concentration of a society's production process.

The level of domestic mobilization can affect the degree of domestic concentration, however. The greater the level of a nation's mobilization for war, the greater the degree of the concentration of its factors of production. In other words, the degree of concentration increases as a function of the level of wartime mobilization. Further, it is assumed here that this increase in the degree of concentration only occurs after a critical threshold has been reached in the mobilization process. This threshold is defined by the full capacity of the society's production base, including the degree of slack not used for current production but available if need be. When the demand generated by the mobilization process exceeds the society's productive capacity, it becomes necessary for there to be changes in the structure of production in order to meet the requirements of wartime mobilization. These changes include an increase in the concentration of the domestic production process. Once the threshold is passed, changes in domestic concentration will be directly related to the degree of wartime mobilization.

> H3: The concentration of production increases as a function of wartime mobilization when that mobilization process exceeds a critical threshold defined by the society's prewar production capacity.

The effects of wartime mobilization on the production process have sometimes been mitigated, however, when governments have consciously undertaken deconcentration policies. During World War II, for example, the Soviet government instituted programs intended to deconcentrate industrial production and disperse population. These policies were defensive measures taken by a nation under attack, and were meant to avoid immediate defeat at Hitler's hands, to prolong the life of the Soviet state for as long as possible. This was, of course, a centrally directed effort, but suggests nonetheless that it is possible for government to act consciously to counteract the natural centralizing and concentrating effects of wartime mobilization.[5] Thus, it appears that wartime increases in governmental concentration, which involve increases in the relative size, scope, and power of the central government, give policy-makers the ability to pursue programs intended to hasten or counteract the increased concentration expected in other aspects of the production process. Governments are natural monopolies that supply the service of protection, and as such they can effect "the extent to which monopoly prevail[s] in other fields of production, and in this way affect human relations throughout the whole economic organization."[6] In other words, increased governmental concentration can itself be an independent determinant of changes in the degree of concentration of the other aspects of the production process.

3

DISTRIBUTION AND INEQUALITY

THE DISCUSSION of war and concentration in the previous chapter emerges from a concern with domestic production processes. In this chapter, the focus of attention is on the flip side of that coin, the process of domestic consumption. One of the major structural aspects of any society is the way in which it distributes various goods to its members. (Again, the term "good" refers here to any desirable, including services, not just to manufactured items.) In any society, those goods are distributed differentially or unequally; not every individual gets the same amount. At least some inequality is a characteristic of all societies, and scholars have focused much attention on its causes and consequences. In this chapter, the emphasis is on changes in the basic level of domestic inequality as a result of war.

The most obvious and most important of the goods that all members of society receive is money. The reason for its importance, of course, is that it is an infinitely flexible medium of exchange; people can purchase almost any other good with money. Thus, the distribution of income often determines the distribution of other goods. More money can be used to buy more and better food, clothing, shelter, transportation, etc. Another good that is distributed among the individual members of a society is status—social rank or standing. Power, the ability to act independently and to control others, is a third differentially distributed good.[1] Like status, power can stem from certain innate attributes, such as physical characteristics, that are not distributed by the society. Nonetheless, power and status are largely socially distributed goods.

The distributions of these three goods, money, power, and status, are highly correlated. For many years, in fact, sociologists studied this covariation with a focus on its consistency. One of their most important measures, S.E.S. (socioeconomic status), combines an individual's social standing and economic well-being. More recently, however, scholars have recognized that there are many individuals whose positions on the various dimensions are inconsistent, and recent research has focused on a search for the determinants and effects of these discrepancies. There is still widespread agreement that the dimensions do covary, however.

The occurrence of war alone is not expected to effect changes in the degree of distributional inequality. It is argued here, however, that wartime mobilization efforts are likely to effect changes in domestic inequality—specifically, that inequality decreases as a function of wartime mobilization via three causal paths. The discussion below, which includes the development of these three links, focuses mainly on income inequality, for this is the most easily quantifiable and measurable of the various dimensions described above. Nevertheless, the argument is developed at a broader level, and suggests that all forms of socially derived inequality are affected by the process of mobilizing for war.

The first link between wartime mobilization and changes in inequality involves the intervening variable of participation.[2] Individuals are one of the resources extracted from society during a wartime mobilization. Indeed, the number of draftees is one way to measure the degree of mobilization. The conscription of individuals and the greater governmental demand for war-related goods lead to an increase in the demand for civilian laborers. In other words, the level of productive participation in the society increases as a direct function of increases in the degree of mobilization. The unemployed, the underemployed, and those not seeking work—those group members who do not participate or do not participate fully in their society's productive processes—find jobs and become productive economic participants. Obviously, participants obtain a greater share of the social product than do nonparticipants. In other words, the income earned by employed individuals is greater than the income of the nonemployed.

As mentioned above, extensive wartime mobilization increases the number of jobs available to those who are counted as unemployed members of the labor force (the jobless actively seeking work). Often, however, many who are not typically counted among the unemployed because they are not actively seeking work, join the labor force during such mobilization efforts. That is, sufficiently large mobilizations increase the productive participation of that group of persons who are not ordinarily counted as members of the labor force, a situation referred to as "negative unemployment." One example is the employment of women in the massive mobilizations of the two world wars. Women not in the labor force, because they neither worked nor sought work, joined the ranks of the employed. The same is true for those minority group members who had given up looking for work because they assumed that they would merely become the subjects of job discrimination.

To the extent that participants obtain more of the social product, domestic inequality decreases as a direct function of the level of mobilization. This is obviously true of income, but also affects the distribution of other goods.[3] The increased participation of women and racial minorities leads to greater status returns as well.[4] An analysis of the impact of World War II on American blacks concludes that "the war had propelled the blacks into the mainstream of American life," and quotes others as saying that the war led "to a new position of the Negro in the United States" and that one result of the war was "a redefinition of the Negro's status."[5]

The other two links between wartime mobilization and changes in inequality involve the nature of the extraction and expenditure processes of a wartime mobilization. Since governments gain control of resources by extracting them from individuals, the progressive or regressive nature of that mobilization can effect changes in inequality. In addition, mobilized resources are utilized for the purpose of waging war, and the ways in which they are expended can also effect changes in inequality.

The second link between mobilization and inequality, then, is the direct effect of extraction. If the resources that are extracted as part of the war effort are those that are differentially distributed among group members, then the extraction process may change the nature of that distribution. Some of the goods that are distributed to group members, such as power and status, are not extracted as part of the mobilization process. Thus, their distribution is affected only indirectly by the society's involvement in conflict; status, for example, is affected through the intervening variable of participation. Individuals, on the other hand, are examples of resources that are extracted but not distributed.[6]

The most obvious example of a good that is both extracted and distributed is money. Governments can obtain money simply by printing it. This creates inflation and leads to an extraction of the purchasing power of individual incomes. Such extraction reduces the degree of inequality, since inflation costs the rich more than the poor. Further, it aids debtors at their creditors' expense.

Most wartime mobilizations also involve extractions through taxation. This too leads to a decrease in inequality, since wartime taxation typically involves a reliance on more direct and progressive taxes than those levied during peace. The reason for this is that abnormally large amounts of resources are extracted from the individuals of a warring nation. Often, it is only possible for governments to achieve the desired level of mobilization through progressive taxation; there is simply not enough income at the bottom to meet government needs. Moreover, since benefits are more obviously linked with costs in wartime, and since benefits are clearly being provided, there is a greater willingness to rely on a relatively greater proportion of direct progressive taxes than in peacetime. Another reason for the institution of progressive tax policies stems from the assumption that the society's elites are aware of the debilitating effect that the increased extraction has on the morale of individual group members and that they want to minimize this effect of mobilization to as great a degree as possible. Thus, it is argued here that many governments, especially democratic ones, will rely more on progressive tax programs during wartime in order to make the sacrifices of individuals seem as equitable as possible. Given that there are more people at the bottom of the income ladder than at the top, the adoption of such policies is one way for governments to try to forestall a breakdown in morale. It appears, however, that such policy decisions may be made in vain, for it is suggested above that wartime cohesion decreases as a function of the absolute level of mobilization rather than as a function of the inequality of the sacrifice.

Governments can also extract resources directly by allocating and rationing goods to individuals and requisitioning from them those goods (i.e., resources) required for the war effort. This extraction procedure also decreases the degree of inequality, since any such rationing system insures a fair distribution by prohibiting the richest from getting all that they want by outbidding those who do not have the resources to compete with them. Thus, the various means of extraction typically employed by governments in wartime lead to decreases in the degree of inequality.

The third link between mobilization and inequality involves the way in which these extracted resources are expended in the war-waging effort. Although there is some dispute as to whether overall government expenditures are progressive or regressive and decrease or increase inequality, there is no disagreement with the statement that government expenditures on social welfare are redistributive.

The provision of social services to those who would otherwise be unable to afford them is one way in which governments redistribute goods among group members. Thus, changes in the amount of the provision of social services effect changes in inequality. The relationship between changes in social service expenditures (one way to measure the level of their provision) and inequality is an inverse one.

Although the relationship between changes in social service provision and inequality is easily apparent, that between the level of mobilization and social service expenditures is not. Again, wartime mobilization involves an increase in the resources that are extracted, expended, and otherwise controlled by national governments. The question that arises is how this increase in extraction affects normal expenditures, specifically those for social services. There are, in fact, two possibilities. The first is that in addition to extracting incremental resources during wartime, governments transfer funds from normal peacetime purposes, such as social services, to the military effort. This suggests, of course, that the entire incremental extraction is used entirely for war purposes and is still insufficient to meet military needs. Rather than extract still more directly, either because the society cannot support greater direct mobilization or for the more likely reason that it will not, governments transfer funds. In this case, therefore, the greater the level of mobilization, the greater the increase in domestic inequality. This case clearly depicts what is termed opportunity costs; there are trade-offs between guns and butter, and greater expenditures for the former lead to fewer expenditures for the latter.

The second possibility is that social services are expanded in wartime, as governments use some of the incremental extraction for nonmilitary purposes. That part of the increased extraction that does go for increased social services is not mobilization per se; rather, the government uses the crisis atmosphere to sneak in additional "peacetime" revenues. The most likely reason for such governmental action, however, is the elite's belief that certain aspects of social service provision may in fact be instrumental to the success of the war effort. The government, may, for example, be greatly concerned about the health of its soldiers and workers, for their well-being is critical to both the

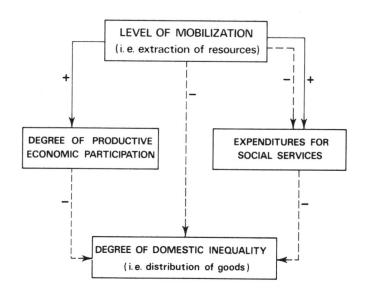

FIGURE 3-1
The Relationships of Wartime Mobilization and Inequality

military and production aspects of the war effort. Another factor with which governments are likely to be concerned in wartime is morale.[7] As suggested above, social cohesion is likely to be negatively affected by the mobilization process. Morale may be affected in much the same way (and is, in fact, one component of an individual's attraction to the group). Yet governments cannot deal with morale problems by ending mobilization. One alternative is for them to attempt to maintain morale by providing social services to those hit hardest by the process of waging war. In this case, therefore, social service expenditures increase as a function of increases in the level of mobilization and thus lead to a decrease in inequality.

Again, the argument presented in this chapter is that wartime mobilization clearly effects changes in the degree of domestic inequality. It is expected that the overall effect of mobilization on inequality is that increases in the degree of the former lead to decreases in the level of the latter.

> H4: Inequality decreases as a function of wartime mobilization through increases in the productive participation of the individual members of society, increases in progressive extraction, and an increase in government expenditures for social services.

The entire relationship is modeled in figure 3–1, where mobilization is seen to affect inequality in three ways. First, there is the indirect link through participation. As the level of mobilization increases, so does the degree of participation; the result is a decrease in the level of domestic inequality. Second, there is the direct link between mobilization and inequality; the extraction of distributed resources (assumed to be progressive) is tentatively posited to be a determinant of a decrease in the degree of inequality. Finally, there is the indirect link between mobilization and inequality through the provision of social services. There are two possibilities here. War may lead to an increase in social service expenditures and a concomitant decrease in inequality, or vice versa. This relationship will be studied in greater detail later.

PART **II**

THE AMERICAN HOMEFRONT IN THE TWENTIETH CENTURY

4

THREAT AND
MOBILIZATION

THE REST of this book is devoted to an examination of the model developed in Part I in order to determine its applicability to real situations— specifically, to the four wars in which the United States has been involved in the twentieth century: World Wars I and II, the Korean War, and the Vietnam War. In addition, these empirical chapters include illustrative evidence from other wars and other nations.

In this chapter, the four cases chosen for intensive investigation are analyzed with particular reference to the independent variables of war and mobilization. These four wars varied greatly along these dimensions; they involved different degrees of threat, and their challenges were met by different levels of mobilization. Thus, the choice of cases provides wide variance for both determinants, an important consideration in the test of any model.[1] Yet these wars also show a number of similarities. In none, for example, was there any extended fighting on American soil, and in none did the United States suffer an outright defeat.[2] The following discussion is divided into two sections; the first deals with the variations in threat perceived during the four conflicts, and the second describes the mobilizations undertaken by the United States in order to wage each war.

THREAT AND AMERICAN WAR
INVOLVEMENT

World War I clearly did not pose an immediate threat to the United States, nor was it widely perceived to do so at the time. When hostilities broke out in Europe in August of 1914, President Wilson pledged that the United States, already counted among the major powers of the world, would maintain a position of neutrality. That stance was, in fact, sustained for the first two and a half years during which war raged in Europe, and when the United States finally adopted the status of belligerent in April 1917, it was not because of any new or cumulative threat to the nation.

Although the official American position on the European war had remained a commitment to neutrality during the first years of the conflict, the people's loyalties were divided but fierce. Different groups of Americans supported both sides in the Continental war, a situation that encouraged the Europeans to respond to the United States' official stand with propaganda campaigns intended to stir American support for one side or the other. At the same time, the belligerents' naval activities constantly challenged Washington's attempts to protect its rights as a neutral nation. But although British actions worried the American government, the Germans' troubled the American people as well.

The German policy of submarine warfare, especially the May 1915 sinking of the Lusitania and the March 1916 sinking of the Sussex, greatly upset most Americans. In each case, the American government responded firmly; it issued a warning to the Germans after the first incident and an ultimatum after the second. Finally, the Germans responded with a public concession to the American position. Yet despite domestic outrage, the American government steadfastly maintained its neutrality and the American people reelected Woodrow Wilson to a second term after he campaigned as the president who "kept us out of war."

Immediately following the election, however, American-German relations were again thrown into crisis. In January 1917, the German government announced the resumption of unrestricted submarine warfare, in violation of the public concession it had offered the previous year. The Americans responded by severing diplomatic relations with Germany. Then, on March 1, the State Department made public an intercepted message that had been sent by the German Foreign Minister, Arthur Zimmerman, to the minister in Mexico. The Zimmerman telegram, as it came to be known, was written to inform the German representative in Mexico that the Germans hoped to enter an alliance with Mexico should the United States join forces with the allies. In return for their commitment to help Mexico "reconquer" Texas, New Mexico, and Arizona, the Germans would expect the Mexicans to declare war on their northern neighbor. Not surprisingly, German-American relations continued to deteriorate. The United States adopted a policy of armed neutrality, but the renewed submarine warfare took its toll. The Germans then sunk three American ships, all bound for the United States, without warning, and President Wilson called Congress into special session. In April 1917, war was declared.

The traditional explanation of America's entry into World War I centered on the German submarine warfare.[3] Later, revisionists did not question that focus, but emphasized the neutrality period instead, arguing that a decided tilt in American policy in favor of the British had left the Germans no choice but to resume unrestricted submarine warfare. Only during World War II, when American society was truly threatened, did Americans offer national security as a reason for the United States entry into World War I. Historians have generally dismissed this view, however: "at no time during the First World War was the United States conscious of fighting a war for survival. . . . no evidence, conclusive beyond reasonable doubt, has been brought to light to show that Wilson . . . was consciously influenced by such considerations or by fear that a German victory might jeopardize American security."[4] Indeed, one historiographic appraisal concludes that "clearly, the hypothesis that the United States went to war in 1917 to protect its security against an immediate threat lacks persuasiveness."[5]

Whereas World War I failed to threaten the United States, American involvement in World War II was a response to a serious threat, one that was perceived at the time and has been questioned only rarely since then.[6] American leaders had watched Asian and European events during the 1930s with trepidation. Afraid at first of again becoming involved in a European war and hoping to remain neutral, they had become convinced by 1941 that the United States could not, and indeed should not, avoid such an involvement. Most American citizens supported actions that might lead the nation into war, and when the Japanese attacked American soil on December 7, 1941, almost all remaining opposition vanished; a united nation, convinced that it was threatened, immediately declared its status as a belligerent.

Although American foreign policy in the interwar period had hardly been isolationist, a majority of Americans had desperately wanted to avoid war, and most at first opposed any actions that might affect American neutrality. When hostilities began in Europe in September 1939, American sentiments were accurately reflected by President Roosevelt's statement, "This nation will remain a neutral nation, but I cannot ask that every American remain neutral in thought as well." Indeed, the commitment to neutrality was so strong during the 1930s that a majority of Americans believed it had been a mistake for the United States to enter World War I.[7]

As German conquests continued apace in Europe, American opinion shifted. By the spring of 1940, over 50 percent of Americans anticipated eventual United States involvement in the European conflict. By summer, 60 percent took that position, and by May 1941, 80 percent agreed. In addition, increasing numbers of Americans were beginning to argue that the nation should become at least somewhat involved. By the second half of 1940, a majority wanted the United States to aid England, even at the risk of getting into the war. By spring 1941, more than 60 percent of Americans took this position.[8]

This shift was also reflected by the growing number of Americans who adopted the view that the American entry into World War I had not been a mistake after all.

This shift in opinion allowed the United States government to increase its support of the Allies. Congress approved the lend-lease program early in 1941, and by September of that year most Americans favored changing the Neutrality Acts in order to allow American merchant ships with American crews to carry war supplies to Britain. By November, more than 60 percent of Americans supported this change.[9] Yet despite the increasing shift of opinion toward active support of the allies, the United States did not become a belligerent until Americans were attacked on their own soil. On December 7, 1941, the Japanese attacked the American naval base at Pearl Harbor and simultaneously attacked Manila, Malaya, Thailand, Hong Kong, and United States island possessions. To the American people, who had become well aware of the German and Japanese appetites for conquest, *the attack on Pearl Harbor confirmed the existence of a threat to the United States*. No longer could they believe that the desires of the dictators would be fulfilled before they reached American shores. Unlike the American declaration of war in 1917, which had been vocally opposed by some senators and representatives, the 1941 resolution was opposed by only a single member of the House. A people that had for as long as possible clung to the hope that they could remain neutral went to war because they had come to believe that their very existence as a nation was threatened.

Like World War I, the Korean War did not directly and immediately threaten the United States, although there was a rationale for entering the conflict. The American nation that emerged from World War II believed that it was responsible for maintaining a peaceful and stable world order. Unlike the period of the 1920s and 1930s, the United States began in the late 1940s to enter alliances and make military commitments. During the five years that followed the end of World War II, American perception of the existence of a cold war with the Soviet Union strengthened, and the United States did not shy away from commitments and actions that opposed Soviet policies. By 1950, these commitments ringed the Soviet Union from Europe to Asia.

On June 25, 1950, the communist government of North Korea invaded the western-oriented South. Korea, which had been divided during the postwar occupation, had not been reunited because of the failure of the great powers to conclude an overall peace settlement at the end of World War II. The North was commited to reuniting the nation under a communist regime. On June 27, President Truman ordered American air and sea forces to aid the beleaguered South Korean troops. Three days later, the American government announced that it had also ordered ground troops to Korea. So began the three-year

American involvement in the Korean War. Although a majority of Americans initially supported the war effort, few suggested that the American involvement was a response to a direct threat to the United States.[10]

Nor was the United States directly and immediately threatened in the Vietnam War. Unlike the Korean War, however, which began with a clear provocation, the invasion of a nation that the United States was commited to support, the American involvement in Vietnam began more tenuously. Indeed, it is difficult even to date precisely the beginning of full-scale American involvement in the war.

Following the Korean War, American commitments to other nations around the globe increased, and American forces were deployed world-wide. Occasionally, the United States became involved in conflicts short of war. When the nation did enter its fourth war of the century, it is not surprising, therefore, that it did so on behalf of a client state, even when it was not itself threatened.

Like Korea, Vietnam had been divided into a communist North and a South oriented toward the western nations. During the early 1960s, the United States slowly became more and more involved in the war between the North and South Vietnamese, but that involvement remained limited largely to an advisory role and support capacity. In 1965, however, the American role shifted to more direct participation, essentially because of United States government fears that the South Vietnamese government was about to collapse. Initially, the new policy of direct participation was limited to the use of American air power in bombing missions on both North and South Vietnamese territory. Soon thereafter, American troops entered ground combat, and by the end of the year the American presence in Vietnam exceeded 180,000 soldiers.

There was clearly no direct threat to the United States stemming from the internal conflict in Vietnam. Moreover, the enemy in this war was not as clearly an aggressor as were the North Koreans, and no distinct event triggered American entry into the war. Few argued that a direct threat did exist. Indeed, unlike World War I and the Korean War, there were not even any events that could be cited to justify or rationalize the American presence in this Southeast Asian conflict. Unlike World War I, no American ships had been sunk, and unlike the Korean War, there had been no direct invasion of the South. Yet it was this war, unthreatening and without clear justification or rationale, that was to be the longest of the four American wars in the twentieth century.

AMERICAN WARTIME MOBILIZATIONS

The following section analyzes the different ways in which the United States mobilized during these four wars, and shows that the cases provide variance for both the rates and amounts of mobilization. The United

TABLE 4-1
The Cost of American Wars in the Twentieth Century

War	Original Incremental Costs (billion $)	National Income in Prewar Year* (billion $)	Original Incremental Cost as % of National Income in Prewar Year
World War I	26.0	36.9	70.5
World War II	288.0	81.1	355.1
Korean War	54.0	217.5	24.8
Vietnam War	107.8	518.1	20.8

Sources: U.S., Bureau of the Census, *Statistical Abstract of the United States: 1975,* 96th ed. (Washington: Government Printing Office, 1975), p. 317, table 510. U.S., Bureau of the Census, *Historical Statistics of the United States, Colonial Times to 1970* (Washington: Government Printing Office, 1976), p. 224, series F7.

*The prewar national income figures are those of the average for 1912–16, 1940, 1949, and 1964, respectively.

States government extracted a wide variety of resources during the process of mobilizing for war, and its policy has generally been to purchase those goods it has needed. Thus, monetary expenditure is a fairly good measure of the level of wartime mobilization. Another such measure is the number of individuals involved in waging war, particularly military personnel.

Clearly, the cumulative mobilization efforts of these four wars varied greatly. An analysis of wartime expenditures reveals that World War II was the costliest American war of the twentieth century, both absolutely and relatively. Despite the inflation of the intervening years, and despite the fact that the American involvement in Vietnam lasted twice as long as it did in World War II, the cost of the Vietnam mobilization, in current dollars, did not even reach half the amount expended between 1941 and 1945. A second estimate of the scope of the cumulative mobilization process, one that is more accurate, can be obtained by computing the cost of waging a war as a fraction of the national income in a prewar year. Of these four conflicts, only World War II cost more than the entire national income for a given year before the war (in this case, 1940). World War I cost more than 70 percent of the average national income from 1912 to 1916. The Korean and Vietnam Wars provide sharp contrast to these estimates, however, for they cost one-quarter and one-fifth, respectively, of the national incomes for 1949 and 1964.[11]

An analysis of the number of individuals who served in the armed forces during each of these periods reinforces the picture of tremendous variation in the levels of these four mobilization efforts. The number of individuals who served in the armed forces during World War II was almost twice the number who served during the Vietnam conflict, almost three times as many as served during the Korean War years, and more than three times as many as served during World War I. Comparing the numbers who served in each war with the population of the United States in each immediately preceding time period

TABLE 4-2
Military Personnel Serving during American Wars in the Twentieth Century

War	Armed Forces Personnel Serving during the War*	Total Prewar American Population (in 1000s)†	% of Prewar Population Serving during the War
World War I	4,734,991	103,414	4.6
World War II	14,903,213	133,402	11.2
Korean War	5,720,000	151,684	3.8
Vietnam War	8,744,000	194,303	4.5

Sources: U.S., Department of Defense, OASD (Comptroller), Directorate for Information Operations and Control, *Selected Manpower Statistics* (Washington: Department of Defense, June 1976), p. 61. U.S., Bureau of the Census, *Historical Statistics of the United States, Colonial Times to 1970* (Washington: Government Printing Office, 1976), p. 8, series A6.

*These totals were computed for the following periods: April 6, 1917 to November 11, 1918; December 1, 1941 to August 31, 1945; June 25, 1950 to July 27, 1953; and August 4, 1964 to January 27, 1973.

†Includes armed forces overseas. The population figures are as of July 1 of the following years: 1917, 1941, 1950, and 1965.

confirms the extent of the World War II mobilization process. More than 10 percent of the American population served in World War II; in no other twentieth-century war did that figure exceed 5 percent. Further, using the numbers of individuals who served during the Korean and Vietnam Wars as a measure of the mobilization efforts undertaken to wage them actually inflates the extent of those extraction processes. The number of individuals who served during World Wars I and II, on the other hand, accurately reflects those wars' mobilization efforts. Before both of the earlier wars, the United States had maintained relatively small peacetime armies (under 200,000 prior to World War I and under 350,000 in 1939). Further, the individuals who served during those conflicts either served in combat or were otherwise directly involved with the war effort. By the outbreak of the Korean War, however, the United States was maintaining peacetime armed forces totaling just under 1.5 million people, and those were stationed in many places besides Korea. Thus, most of those serving in the armed forces during the Korean War were not in Korea and were not likely to be sent there. Rather, they served in capacities not even related to the ongoing conflict. Following the war, American military commitments continued to increase, and by the mid-1960s, the American armed forces numbered more than 2.5 million individuals stationed around the world. During the war period, most of the 8.5 million individuals serving in the military were not, in fact, in Vietnam, or any other part of Southeast Asia. The total number of people who served in the entire region was 3,403,100 (1.8 percent of the total prewar population). In Vietnam itself, 2,594,200 (1.3 percent of the total prewar population) served.[12] Thus, the cumulative military personnel figures exaggerate the mobilizations undertaken to wage the Korean and Vietnam Wars.

These four wars also varied greatly in length. Direct American participation in World War I lasted only nineteen months, whereas it lasted for ninety-three months in Vietnam. Thus, the resources extracted during these wars were mobilized over different periods of time.

Finally, these wars varied not only in the degree of the extraction process but in the rates of their mobilizations as well. Plotting the annual total of United States military personnel on active duty in the twentieth century reveals that the first three wars display the same basic pattern. In each of these wars, mobilization increased very quickly during the beginnings of the conflict period and then continued to increase at a slower rate until the end of the war.[13] In Vietnam, on the other hand, the American mobilization peaked early, in 1969, before the end of the war, and then decreased steadily. This trend reflects President Nixon's policy of Vietnamization, the phased withdrawal of American ground combat personnel.[14]

Thus, these four conflicts display a variety of patterns for the independent

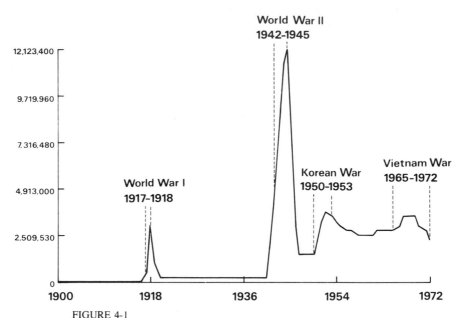

FIGURE 4-1
Total U.S. Military Personnel on Active Duty, 1900–1972
   Sources: U.S., Bureau of the Census, *Historical Statistics of the United States, Colonial Times to 1970* (Washington: Government Printing Office, 1976), p. 1141, series Y904. U.S., Department of Defense, OASD (Comptroller), Directorate for Information Operations and Control, *Selected Manpower Statistics* (Washington: Department of Defense, June 1976), p. 20.

TABLE 4-3
The Duration of American Wars in the Twentieth Century

War	Date of War Entry	Date Hostilities Terminated	Length (in months)
World War I	April 6, 1917 President signs war declaration	November 11, 1918 Armistice signed	19
World War II	December 8, 1941 President signs war declaration	September 2, 1945 V-J Day, Japan surrenders (V-E Day: May 8, 1945)	46
Korean War	June 30, 1950 President orders in American troops	July 27, 1953 Armistice into effect	37
Vietnam War	May 3, 1965 American troops land in Vietnam	January 27, 1973 Ceasefire into effect	93

variables of threat and mobilization. Only when the nation is directly attacked does all of its citizenry perceive a real threat to its physical and territorial integrity. Only World War II involved such a direct and immediate threat to the United States. The other three conflicts involved lesser degrees of threat, if any, but were justified and rationalized in a variety of ways. Further, the rates and cumulative amounts of extraction varied greatly, as did the duration of the mobilization processes during these four conflicts.

5

DOMESTIC DISUNITY

THIS CHAPTER evaluates the propositions developed in chapter 1 relating the onset of war and the process of mobilization to changes in the level of domestic cohesion. It does so in the context of the United States' involvement in the four wars discussed above.

Thus, it is necessary to have continuous longitudinal data on domestic cohesion.[1] The common strategy, however, is to measure cohesion by measuring the lack of it. Behavioral studies, especially those of large groups, generally evaluate changes in cohesion by focusing on changes in the manifestation of behaviors that evince a lack of cohesion. Studies of disaster situations, for example, often measure the degree of cohesion by looking at the extent of panic behavior. In small group studies, on the other hand, researchers measure the degree of conflict and assume direct inverse covariation between changes in conflict behavior and group cohesion. Thus, data have been gathered on several indicators, or manifestations, of the lack of cohesion for as many years as possible.[2] A composite measure of domestic disunity, obtained by combining these indicators, provides the basis for this chapter's analysis of war and domestic cohesion. In addition, this chapter includes supplementary evidence on discord in the United States and other countries, as well as secondary discussions of the indicants themselves. Plausible rival hypotheses are also discussed.

CRIME

Crime, by definition, is behavior that breaks group norms, and at least some crime occurs in every society. Although there is an abundance of

38

theories that explain criminal motivation, and although such motivations may vary, it is nonetheless apparent that criminal behavior evinces some degree of dissatisfaction with the society in addition to whatever else it may tell us about the criminal. Crime then, is one manifestation of discord, and changes in the amount of crime can be used as one measure of changes in the degree of domestic discord.

In this project, annual data on the violent crime rate in the United States from 1935 to 1972 provide one such measure.[3] Although using the crime rate does control for changes in the size of the population, it does not control for changes in the size of the most criminally prone population, those young people between the ages of fifteen and twenty-four.[4] If this is not done, a plausible rival hypothesis can be offered to explain the crime wave of the 1960s, when the children of the baby boom entered the criminally prone age bracket.[5] Thus, the violent crime rate was calculated controlling for the resident youth age population[6] (see figure 5-5) and is used as an indicant of fluctuation in societal discord.

STRIKES

The second indicator of domestic disunity employed here is the number of yearly strikes, or work stoppages, in the United States.[7] Strikes, like crime, have been studied by scholars in a number of disciplines and in many different ways. There appears to be a consensus among these scholars that strike behavior is indeed a manifestation of domestic conflict. Although strikes may not necessarily break group norms (especially if the society accords them legitimacy on a general, if not case-by-case, level), they clearly evince dissatisfaction on the part of workers. When strikes occur in wartime, they are especially significant, for they can affect the entire war effort. It is for precisely this reason that societies often take special precautions to prevent the occurrence of strikes during wartime.

In some wars, strikes have been outlawed, and some governments have established special agencies to deal with labor problems during periods of conflict. During World War I, for example, President Woodrow Wilson established the National War Labor Board. A similar agency was established in World War II as well. In addition, the leaders of organized labor have sometimes pledged that their unions would not go on strike during war years. Both the American Federation of Labor and the Congress of Industrial Organizations made such no-strike pledges and promised to "produce without interruption" during World War II. When damaging strikes do occur in periods of conflict, governments often enact repressive legislation to curb them. In 1943, for example, the United States Congress passed the War Labor Dispute Act over the president's veto.

TABLE 5-1
Discord in the U.S., Principal Components Analysis, 1935–72

	Unrotated Factor Loadings
Violent crime rate, controlled for size of young adult population (per 100,000 people ages 15–24)	.91
Number of strikes	.76
Number of domestic violence events	.77

Sources: Figure 5-5. U.S., Bureau of the Census, *Historical Statistics of the United States, Colonial Times to 1970* (Washington: Government Printing Office, 1976), p. 179, series D970, D977. Michael Steven Stohl, ''War and Domestic Political Violence in the United States 1890–1970: The American Capacity for Repression and Reaction'' (Ph.D. dissertation, Northwestern University, 1974), p. 196, appendix III. U.S., Department of Labor, Bureau of Labor Statistics, *Monthly Labor Review* 96 (September 1973): 133.
Program: W. J. Dixon, ed., *BMDP Biomedical Computer Programs* (Berkeley and Los Angeles: University of California Press, 1975), program P4M.

Briefly, therefore, the existence of war often means that the expression of worker dissatisfaction takes on added significance. Given these concerted attempts by both government and labor to prevent wartime strikes, any work stoppages during wartime, not least if their occurrence is more common than before the war, can certainly be interpreted as manifesting an increase in social discord. Thus, the annual number of strikes in the United States during the twentieth century is employed here as a second indicator of domestic disunity.

DOMESTIC CONFLICT EVENTS

Students of both domestic and international conflict have recently begun to create historical data bases of conflictual events rather than to rely on the aggregate data provided by government agencies and bureaus. One such collection includes continuous annual data on the number of violent domestic events in the United States between 1935 and 1970, where domestic political violence is defined ''as all collective nongovernmental or governmental attacks on persons or property resulting in damage to them that occur within the boundaries of an autonomous political system.''[8] These data provide the third indicator of domestic disunity.

DOMESTIC DISUNITY

When combined, these three indicators provide a single index for the annual degree of domestic disunity since the years prior to World War II. One way to create this index is by using a principle components analysis without rotation, a procedure that is based on the logic of shared variation, to combine the data on crime, strikes, and domestic conflict. The factor scores that emerge provide the index of the underlying concept (or factor) of domestic disunity, an index that can be used to evaluate the propositions developed in chapter 1. Table 5-1 presents the factor loadings for each of the three variables in the principle components analysis. Figure 5-1 displays the factor scores that are obtained for the years 1935 to 1972.[9] Using these, it is possible to analyze directly changes in domestic discord that occur as a result of war and mobilization. The pattern that emerges from this data clearly reveals the effects of American involvements in war on the movement of the series. Quite simply, cohesion decreased in all three wars.

The hypotheses developed in chapter 1 entail twin expectations. Certain wars, those that involve threat, are expected to effect an initial increase in cohesion. This pattern would be expected to fit World War II. Nonthreatening wars, however, such as the Korean or Vietnam conflicts, are not expected to show this initial decrease in disaffection. Moreover, cohesion is expected to have decreased during the course of all three wars. In order to test these predictions, separate trend lines have been fitted to all nonwar periods, wartime values regressed on the level of mobilization as measured by the number of military personnel, and dummy variables included to estimate the step-level changes that occur at the cutting points, the points at which wars begin and end. The cutting points in this regression were chosen in order to maximize

FIGURE 5-1
Discord in the U.S., 1935-72. Factor Scores from Principal Components Analysis (from table 5-1)

TABLE 5-2
Discord in the U.S., Results of Interrupted Time-Series Analysis Incorporating Mobilization, 1935–72

Variables	Estimated Coefficient (t-statistics in parentheses)	
Original intercept	−1.04	(5.0)
Pre–World War II trend	−.002	(.04)
Step-level change at outset of World War II	−.07	(.2)
World War II: 100,000 military personnel*	.008	(3.1)
Step-level change after World War II	−.71	(2.5)
Interwar trend: slope change from last nonwar period	.24	(1.9)
Step-level change at outset of Korean War	−.33	(.51)
Korean War: 100,000 military personnel*	.011	(.64)
Step-level change after Korean War	−.84	(3.0)
Interwar trend: slope change from last nonwar period	−.19	(1.6)
Step-level change at outset of Vietnam War	−3.19	(3.8)
Vietnam War: 100,000 military personnel*	.154	(5.9)

*Variables lagged one year.
Procedure: Generalized least squares with iteration that is maximum likelihood.
Estimate of serial correlation = −.24.
R^2 = .96.
Program: John K. Peck, *Yale TSP: Time Series Processor,* version 4.4 (New Haven, Conn.: Yale University, Department of Economics, August 1975).

fit, as was the specification of a one-year lag for the military personnel regressor. Specifying the model in this way provides an assessment both of any step-level changes that occur in the series immediately upon war entry, and of the covariation of wartime changes in cohesion with wartime levels of mobilization. The results of this interrupted time-series analysis are presented in table 5–2, and the fitted values from the regression are presented in figure 5–2.

The results obtained from this regression do not show a step-level decrease in the series occasioned by the onset of war.[10] The results of this time-series regression clearly reveal, however, the effects of mobilization on domestic cohesion. In all three wars, the sign and magnitude of the coefficients confirm expectations, as does the ordering of the coefficients across the wars. Clearly, mobilization is associated with increased manifestations of the lack of cohesion. Except for the Korean War, the coefficient estimates are highly significant.[11] Moreover, the actual sizes of the coefficients are quite revealing.[12] Given that World War II was the only one of the four wars to involve a threat to American society, it is not surprising that the marginal propensity for decreased cohesion was smallest in this conflict. In the Korean War, the marginal propensity for decreased cohesion was also fairly small. The coefficient that is obtained for the American involvement in Vietnam, on the other hand, is fourteen times the coefficient for the Korean War and nineteen times the coefficient for World War II. Thus, the different characteristics of these conflicts are visible not in the step-level changes they effect in the series, but in the marginal effects of their mobilization processes. The World War II mobilization, at least twice the size of that imposed during the years of the American involvement in Vietnam, had one-nineteenth the impact on domestic cohesion!

It is also apparent that wartime discord peaked in the last year of the Korean conflict and in the year following the end of World War II. In both cases, the level of domestic cohesion then increased sharply after the reestablishment of peace. Neither postwar reequilibration involved a return to prewar levels of cohesion, however. Rather, discord leveled off at a point higher than that which existed prior to the war, but lower than the war-effected peak. In the Vietnam War case, the data reflect the Nixon administration's policy of Vietnamization as a means of withdrawing American troops while sustaining the basic war effort through the use of indigenous soldiers. One result of this policy was to mitigate the decrease in domestic cohesion that the mobilization process had effected. In this instance, the disunity curve matches the mobilization curve with a one-year lag ($r = .90$). This suggests that the process by which mobilization affects cohesion works in both directions: that manifestations of the lack of cohesion increase with increases in the level of mobilization and decrease with decreases in mobilization.

FIGURE 5-2
Discord in the U.S., Fitted Values of Time-Series Regression Analysis, 1935–72 (from regression analysis presented in table 5-2)

SUPPORTING MATERIALS

In addition to the data analyzed above, there is additional evidence, not amenable to these estimation techniques, that also supports the propositions developed in chapter 1. Table 5-3, for example, presents data on the number of racial disturbances in the United States from 1900 to 1967. These data reveal that 190 of the 210 disturbances occurred during five-year periods that were marked by wars during much of their span. There were large numbers of racial disturbances in the United States during World Wars I and II and the Vietnam War. Only during the period of the American involvement in Korea were there no racial disturbances.

Another kind of illustrative evidence is public opinion data, a somewhat more direct measure of American sentiments during wartime. John Mueller's work on public support of American war efforts shows clearly that such backing declined during the Korean and Vietnam conflicts. Interestingly, Mueller found the largest determinant of this decline to be the cumulative number of American battle casualties (measured logarithmically). Mueller employed this particular indicant not because it represented some larger process (e.g., mobilization), but because he found that it was a direct target of public reaction. Americans knew and cared how many soldiers were dying during these wars. In this project, the focus is not explicitly on public feelings about loss of life during conflict, but on the impact on Americans of the sacrificial burdens they have carried in wartime—including but not limited to the cost in life. Although battle deaths and other measures of mobilization often covary,[13] Mueller's use of a *cumulative* measure represents a different conceptualization of the process by which mobilization is translated into disaffection than the one employed here. Indeed, his findings do not show an increase in the level of support for the Vietnam War following the institutionalization of the Vietnamization program. Rather, his data reveal that support for the war continued to drop through May 1971, where his analysis ends. It would be interesting to know what a continuation of the analysis would show for the last years of the war. Another of Mueller's results squares better with the results obtained here, however. A brief glance at his data reveals that there was a larger marginal effect of battle casualties on American support for the Vietnam than the Korean War. The difference he finds is not of the same order of magnitude as that shown here, probably because he used the logarithm of the independent variable. Finally, Mueller's remark that World War II, "although unquestionably much more highly supported by the public than the Korean and Vietnam Wars, seems to have been rather less consensual than might be supposed," certainly fits with the results discussed above.[14]

In addition, congressional voting patterns provide a third illustration of the effects of war on domestic cohesion. Given their status as representatives of the American people, the members of Congress can be assumed to reflect (or

TABLE 5-3
Collective Racial Violence in the U.S., 1900–1967

Five-Year Periods	Disturbances*	Five-Year Periods	Disturbances*
1900–1904	1	1935–1939	1
1905–1909	2	1940–1944	18
1910–1914	0	1945–1949	0
1915–1919	22	1950–1954	0
1920–1924	4	1955–1959	0
1925–1929	1	1960–1964	11
1930–1934	0	1965–1967	150

Source: Warren Schaich, "A Relationship Between Collective Racial Violence and War," Journal of Black Studies 5 (June 1975): 379.
*Disturbances only include riots resulting in personal injury, or loss of life, or arrests, or property damage.

to lead) the sentiments of their constituencies. Thus, divisions within Congress are indicative of divisions within the broader population, and the degree of congressional bipartisanship can be used as another indicator of domestic cohesion. Because bipartisanship represents the willingness of the minority party to support governmental policies, a high level of such cooperation during wartime (both on war and nonwar issues) suggests an unwillingness on the part of the opposition to hamper the war and mobilization efforts in any way. Indeed, yearly data on congressional voting during World War II reveals a dramatic drop in partisanship from 1941 to 1942.[15] Just as clearly evident, however, is the increase in partisan behavior during 1943. For the rest of the war, partisanship remained at this higher level. These data are presented in table 5-4.

A longer data series on congressional partisanship is also available. A scatterplot of these data clearly reveals a downward trend in partisanship over

TABLE 5-4
U.S. Congress, Partisanship, 1941–45

Year	Percentage of Votes in Which a Majority of Democrats Opposed a Majority of Republicans		Percentage of Votes Which Were Not Unanimous	
	House	Senate	House	Senate
1941	56.25	70.6	96.25	92.6
1942	26.4	34.0	84.7	90.4
1943	51.6	53.0	91.2	97.5
1944	44.6	53.0	89.3	96.9
1945	50.0	52.9	98.6	99.0

Source: Calculated from data provided by Roland Young, Congressional Politics in the Second World War (New York: Columbia University Press, 1956; reprint ed., New York: Da Capo Press, 1972), p. 269, table B.

the course of the twentieth century. Independent of this secular decline, how-ever, is a clear drop in partisanship during World War I. It was during this period, in fact, that the percentage of party votes in a given Congress (two-year period) dropped below 50 percent for the first time in the century. Unfortunately, however, there is only a single war observation for this con-flict.

During World War II, the data show the same pattern as the yearly data discussed above. The first wartime Congress (January 1941 to December 1942) was very bipartisan; the percentage of party votes (43 percent) set a new century low. It marked a substantial drop in partisanship from the last prewar Congress, which divided along party lines 71 percent of the time. The Korean pattern does not fit expectations, however. The drop in partisanship did not occur until the second war Congress and was not followed by renewed party squabbles. The Vietnam pattern is much like that of World War II; a drop in partisanship in the first war Congresses is followed by an increase.

It appears that the onset of war is generally followed by an initial drop in partisanship. This drop occurred in all four wars, even the nonthreatening ones, and the pattern is more marked and visible than those of the other measures of disunity. The difference between this political manifestation

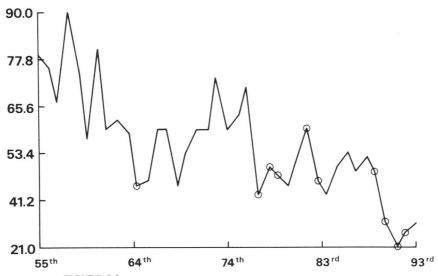

FIGURE 5-3
Partisanship* in the U.S. Congress, House of Representatives, 55th–93rd Congresses†

○ = War congresses. *Percentage of party votes. †Period of session: 55th from March 1897 to March 1899; 93rd from January 1973 to December 1974.
    Source: Jerome M. Clubb and Santa Traugott, ''Partisan Cleavage and Cohesion in the House of Representatives, 1861–1974,'' *Journal of Interdisciplinary History* 7 (Winter 1977): 383, table 1.

of the lack of cohesion and the other indicants suggests that factors other than war itself also affect political behavior in such a way as to mitigate the partisan behavior that indicates the disaffection of office-holders. Clearly, the political opposition must avoid appearing unpatriotic during the initial stages of war, even when no threat is involved. Even if such behavior does not affect the course of war, the political liabilities of "failing" to support troops in combat deter opposition politics. Thus, the drop in partisanship is more marked and the later increase more muted; political limits remain in effect for the full duration of war.[16]

The same basic pattern of changes in the level of domestic cohesion can also be seen in the wartime experiences of Great Britain. The indictable crime rate (controlled for the size of the youth population) and the annual number of strikes in Great Britain were combined to provide annual factor scores of British disunity; these scores are displayed in figure 5-4. The indictable crime rate increased during World War I (the 1918 figure is 134 percent of that for 1913) and increased even more dramatically in World War II (the 1945 crime rate was 244 percent of that for 1938). The annual number of strikes in Britain decreased slightly during the first years of World War I, reached their low point in 1916, and then began to climb, peaking in 1919. No similar dip is evident for the first part of World War II but, given the steady increase in strikes before the conflict began, it is significant that the annual number of strikes leveled off with the onset of war. The number of annual strikes then began to climb again, peaking in 1945. The factor scores (figure 5-4) show no dip during the beginning of World War II, although the increase in that series is less than might be expected given the prewar trend. The factor score pattern for World War I shows an initial decline that bottoms out with the 1916 observation, followed by an increase that peaks at 1919.

SECONDARY DISCUSSIONS OF STRIKES AND CRIME

The relationship between the involvement of a nation in war and the pattern of its strike activities has been noted by others. One comparative analysis of the wartime experiences of the four major belligerent nations in World War I, for example, reveals that three of them (Germany, France, and England) suffered fewer work stoppages during the initial stages of the war than in the immediate prewar period.[17] After the initial decrease, however, the number of annual strikes in each of these nations rose steadily for the rest of the war and then peaked after the conflict ended. The fourth major belligerent, the United States, also experienced an increase in strikes during the short time it was involved in the war. In the three European nations, the increase in strikes during the war occurred despite the institutionalization of repressive measures designed to curb work stoppages and the drastic penalties that were

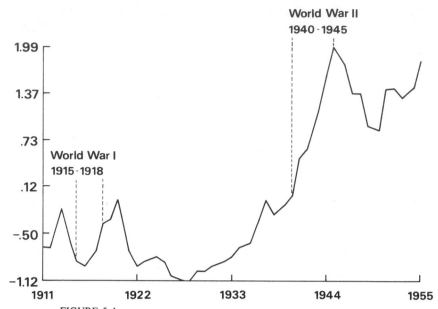

FIGURE 5-4
Discord in Great Britain, 1911–55 (factor scores from principal components analysis)

Unrotated
factor loadings

Indictable crime rate, controlled for size of resident civilian young adult population
    (ages 15–24) .95
Number of work stoppages .95

Sources: B. R. Mitchell and H. G. Jones, *Second Abstract of British Historical Statistics* (London: Cambridge University Press, 1971), pp. 201–2. Great Britain, General Register Office, *Annual Report of the Registrar-General of Births, Deaths, and Marriages in England and Wales,* vols. 74(1911)–83(1920) (London: H.M. Stationery Office, 1913–21). Great Britain, General Register Office, *The Registrar-General's Statistical Review of England and Wales for the Years 1921–1930: Text,* New Annual Series Nos. 1–10 (London: H.M. Stationery Office, 1923–32). Great Britain, General Register Office, *The Registrar-General's Statistical Review of England and Wales for the Years 1931–1955: Tables Part I Medical* (London: H.M. Stationery Office, 1933–56). George Sayer Bain, Robert Bacon, and John Pimlott, "The Labour Force," in *Trends in British Society Since 1900: A Guide to the Changing Social Structure of Britain,* ed. A. H. Halsey (London: Macmillan, 1972), pp. 127–28, table 4.14.

Notes: The resident youth population figures for 1916–20 were estimated using data provided by the sources. Arthur M. Ross and Paul T. Hartman, eds., *Changing Patterns of Industrial Conflict* (New York: John Wiley and Sons, 1960), p. 194, table A-1, exclude the 1926 General Strike. B. R. Mitchell, *European Historical Statistics 1750–1970* (New York: Columbia University Press, 1975), p. 177, table C3, includes strikes in Southern Ireland for 1911 and 1912, and contains an error for 1924.

then imposed on a number of occasions. In Germany, the increase in strikes was, in fact, the impetus for the passage of an act subjecting all workers to industrial conscription. Nonetheless, the annual number of strikes did not decline.

Many of the studies that analyze the determinants of work stoppages have pointed to the independent effect of war. The French involvements in World Wars I and II have been accurately viewed as watersheds in the developmental patterns of that nation's strike activities.[18] Studies analyzing the economic determinants of work stoppages in the United States have been unsuccessful in explaining the occurrence of strikes, and have noted the wartime deviations in strike patterns. One such study divided American strike activity into two separate time periods because there was a lack of correspondence between the number of strikes and the business cycle for the years from 1939 to 1950. One important reason for this discrepancy is that war affected the series, leading the author to the conclusion that "political events" such as "the sharp impact of Pearl Harbor" influence the number of strikes and "account for many deviations from the normal cyclical pattern."[19] A second study of the relationship between economic fluctuations and strike patterns argues that "changes in strikes apparently have occurred on three levels," and that "the two world wars very likely affected all three kinds of movements. Generally, we have not made too much effort to explain the war developments."[20]

The relationship between war and crime has been more generally recognized than that between conflict and strikes, and scholars generally agree that the two are "closely interwoven."[21] This close connection is starkly displayed in figure 5-5, which presents the violent crime rate in the United States, controlled for the size of the resident young adult population. The impact of war involvement appears to have been the central factor driving the changes in the series between 1935 and 1972.[22]

Analyses of crime in different nations and wars have found that crime generally increases either during a nation's involvement in war or shortly thereafter.[23] Although some scholars offer economic explanations for the crime trend, close scrutiny of the evidence reveals no consistent relationship.[24] Crimes have increased both in nations where war has brought prosperity and where it has caused economic hardship. It has been noted, on the other hand, that "the initial stage of a war is one of general enthusiasm, a wave of patriotic sentiments, and a consequent decline in crime. . . . After a few months of elation much of that wave of enthusiasm disappears, and the crime figures begin to rise."[25] This pattern, identical to the one noted here, has been termed "axiomatic" by one author and a "fairly widespread tendency" by another.[26]

A pathbreaking study by Archer and Gartner that compares the prewar and postwar homicide rates of both belligerent and nonbelligerent nations also provides fascinating evidence about the relationship of war and cohesion. Taking five-year averages in the homicide rates for both prewar and postwar periods, the authors find that belligerent nations were more likely to have experienced postwar increases than were nonbelligerent nations.[27] They reject an economic explanation for this pattern since they find that postwar homicide rates increased in nations whose economies were both weakened and strengthened by their involvements in war.

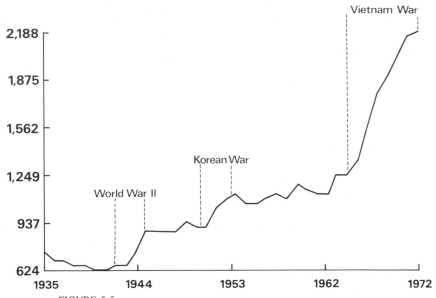

FIGURE 5-5
Violent Crime Rate in the U.S., Controlled for Size of Resident Young Adult Population, 1935-72 (rate per 100,000 persons ages 15-24, excluding armed forces overseas)

Sources: U.S., Executive Office of the President: Office of Management and Budget, *Social Indicators 1973* (Washington: Government Printing Office, 1973), p. 64, table 2/1. U.S., Bureau of the Census, *Historical Statistics of the United States, Colonial Times to 1970* (Washington: Government Printing Office, 1976), p. 10, series A32. U.S., Bureau of the Census, "Estimated Population of the United States, by Age, Color, and Sex: 1940 to 1946," *Population—Special Reports,* series P-47, no. 3 (April 3, 1947). U.S., Bureau of the Census, "Estimates of the Population of the United States, by Age, Color, and Sex: 1946 to 1948," *Current Population Reports,* series P-25, no. 21 (May 27, 1949), p. 7. U.S., Bureau of the Census, "Estimates of the Population of the Continental United States, by Age, Color, and Sex: July 1, 1947 to 1949," *Current Population Reports,* series P-25, no. 39 (May 5, 1950), pp. 5-6. U.S., Bureau of the Census, "Estimates of the Population of the United States and Components of Change, by Age, Color, and Sex: 1950-1960," *Current Population Reports,* series P-25, no 310 (June 30, 1965), p. 11. U.S., Bureau of the Census, "Estimates of the Population of the United States, by Age, Sex, and Race: April 1, 1960 to July 1, 1973," *Current Population Reports,* series P-25, no. 519 (April 1974), pp. 12-53.

Of great interest here is their finding that those nations that suffered a high number of battle casualties more typically experienced increases in their homicide rates than did nations with lower numbers of troop deaths. This finding can be offered as additional supporting evidence for the proposition developed in chapter 1 that cohesion decreases during the course of war as a function of mobilization. The empirical work presented earlier in this chapter indicates that disunity does not actually peak until the first year after a war ends, and that there is then a reequilibration at a level higher than before the war. Thus, it is expected that postwar discord would be relatively higher in those nations that had experienced higher levels of mobilization than in those that had not mobilized to the same extent—exactly the pattern that Archer and Gartner find.[28]

PLAUSIBLE RIVAL HYPOTHESES

The most plausible alternative explanation for changes in the level of domestic disunity or its manifestations might seem to be economic.[29] As noted above, however, studies of the relationship of economic fluctuations to the occurrence of strikes have found that wartime patterns do not often fit expectations derived from the business cycle. Similarly, economic factors have been rejected as an explanation for the occurrence of racial violence in the United States during the twentieth century.[30] Further, the most recent studies of the relationship between economic conditions, especially unemployment, and crime have found that none indeed exists.[31]

A more plausible determinant of changes in domestic cohesion is domestic concentration.[32] It may be that wartime decreases in cohesion are not a function of the burdens of extraction but of the turmoil and upheaval of migration and population redistribution. In explaining changes in the violent crime rate, for example, this rival hypothesis predicts that it should not increase uniformly in all regions of a nation during wartime, but that increases would be expected to occur only in those areas that experience large in-migrations. Disaggregating crime data is one way to control for this rival hypothesis. If general sacrifice is the key determinant of changes in domestic cohesion, then increases in the violent crime rate should be evidenced in all regions of a nation and in all communities, regardless both of their size and of net changes in their population due to migration. If, on the other hand, the turmoil and dislocation that accompany mobilization are at work here, then the increases in the violent crime rate should be greatest in those regions experiencing the greatest growth and upheaval. A regional analysis of the violent crime rate in the United States during World War II shows that the rival hypothesis does not successfully explain the decrease in cohesion that occurred during that period,

TABLE 5-5
Increase in U.S. Violent Crime Rate (Excluding Rape) by Region and City Size, 1940–46

Region	% Increase	Net Migration (in 1000s)
New England	37.4	+423
Middle Atlantic	26.6	−68
East North Central	19.0	+954
West North Central	93.5	−693
South Atlantic	53.9	−580
East South Central	19.0	−1178
West South Central	54.8	−763
Mountain	120.7	−229
Pacific	107.4	+2920

The increase in the violent crime rate is calculated using the civilian population recorded by the 1940 census, and the estimated civilian population for 1946 not including those born between 1940 and 1946.

Population Groups	% Increase	Population Groups	% Increase
Group I: cities over 250,000	31.4	Group IV: 25,000 to 50,000	42.8
Group II: 100,000 to 250,000	41.2	Group V: 10,000 to 25,000	36.7
Group III: 50,000 to 100,000	31.9	Group VI: cities under 10,000	32.7

Sources: U.S., Department of Justice, Federal Bureau of Investigation, *Uniform Crime Reports for the United States and its Possessions* 11 (January 1941): 161, 173, 175, tables 76, 80, 81. U.S., Department of Justice, Federal Bureau of Investigation, *Uniform Crime Reports for the United States and its Possessions* 17 (January 1947): 81, 88–91, tables 28, 30. U.S., Bureau of the Census, "Estimated Population of the United States, by Regions, Divisions, and States: July 1, 1946," *Current Population Reports*, series P-25, no. 2 (August 15, 1947), pp. 3–4, tables 1, 2.

which involved the greatest degree of mobilization and wartime migration of the four wars studied here. Thus, the rival hypothesis would be expected to be most applicable to this case, and if disconfirmed here, can be assumed to be generally falsified.

As table 5-5 clearly reveals, communities of every size experienced increases in violent crime, as did every region of the country. In other words, there is no relationship between in-migration and the violent crime rate.[33] The rejection of this rival hypothesis is bolstered by the work of others as well. Two studies of the relationship of urbanization and population density to the occurrence of violent crime find that no such relationship in fact exists.[34] Similarly, migration has been ruled out as a determinant of racial disturbances in the United States during the twentieth century.[35]

SUMMARY

The empirical work presented in this chapter provides strong evidence in support of the hypotheses developed above in chapter 1. It does not, however, validate them by significantly rejecting the null hypothesis. Nor does it reject all plausible rival models. Rather, it shows that the cases analyzed, as well as evidence provided by the work of others, do conform to the expectations that this model suggests.

The fundamental conclusion here is that domestic cohesion decreases during wartime as a function of the process of mobilization, despite any positive effects the war may have in bringing a society together. Even when individuals in a nation believe that the nation's existence is threatened and that a common struggle can successfully meet that challenge, their society will suffer the fragmenting effects of the mobilization process. It seems that the more important effect of the existence of threat is not necessarily in increasing cohesion at a war's beginning, but in slowing wartime increases in domestic disunity. In other words, the existence of threat leads to a smaller propensity for increased discord given the size of a particular mobilization. This is graphically illustrated by the American experiences during the Vietnam War and World War II. Despite the relatively small mobilization undertaken to wage the Vietnam War, there was a tremendous decrease in domestic cohesion. During World War II, on the other hand, cohesion decreased only slightly, despite the massive size of the mobilization effort.

6

CENTRALIZATION AND CONCENTRATION

WHEN WARTIME mobilization exceeds a certain threshold, it increases the degree of domestic concentration. Where that threshold lies depends on the prewar production structure and the amount of slack capacity available. Briefly, the greater the burden of wartime extraction given the society's prewar production base, the greater the likelihood that changes in the structure of production will be necessary in order to effectively wage war.

The wartime mobilizations undertaken by the United States during the twentieth century have varied both in absolute size and as a proportion of the society's prewar production. In table 4–1, the original incremental costs of the four wars are compared with the prewar production base measured here by annual national income.[1] In this respect, World Wars I and II were markedly different from the Korean and Vietnam Wars. Those differences are magnified in a comparison of average yearly incremental costs and average yearly prewar national incomes. As shown in table 6–1, World War II again appears to have involved the largest mobilization effort of these four conflicts. The average annual cost of waging that war was 92.6 percent of the entire national income for 1940. The average annual cost of World War I was 44 percent of the average yearly national income for the years 1912–16. By contrast, the Korean War's average yearly cost was only 8 percent of the national income for 1949, and the Vietnam War's average yearly cost was only 2.7 percent of the national income for 1964. It seems likely, therefore, that the mobilizations undertaken during the two world wars exceeded the critical threshold and thus served to increase the degree of domestic concentration. The mobilizations for the Korean and Vietnam Wars, on the other hand, hardly seem large enough to have necessitated changes in the way American society was organized for production in order to accomodate the added burdens of wartime.

These four wars show similar variation in the effects of their mobilization processes on the size and scope of government. In World Wars I and II, the average annual extraction of resources exceeded the total amount of resources controlled by the government prior to the war. Both the total cost of World War II, $288 billion, and its average annual cost, $75.1 billion, exceeded the total expenditures of the United States government in 1940, $9.589 billion. The average annual cost of World War I exceeded by twenty-three times the entire amount expended by the United States government in 1916.

In sharp contrast to the two world wars, both the total and average annual costs of the Vietnam War never exceeded the annual prewar expenditures of the federal government. The total cost of that conflict, $107.8 billion spent over seven and one half years, was over $10 billion less than the total federal budget for 1964. Indeed, the average annual cost of the Vietnam War came to only one-quarter of the prewar expenditures on defense and national security. Even the highest yearly cost of the war, some $30 billion, was only slightly more than one-half the prewar expenditures on defense and national security. The total cost of the three-year long involvement in Korea did exceed the total prewar expenditures of the federal government. The average annual cost was less than one-half the total annual prewar expenditures on national defense, however.

The American war mobilizations in World Wars I and II were massive, entailing the extraction of resources that constituted a large proportion of societal production. They also exceeded the prewar size and scope of the federal government. If ever the requisites of mobilization have required a change in the structure of a society's production process, then the world wars met those requirements. The mobilizations for the Korean and Vietnam Wars were relatively small by contrast; both efforts were within the scope of the society's prewar productive capacity and the government's extractive and allocative capacities. Thus, no increase in domestic concentration would be expected to have occurred in these two conflicts. For World Wars I and II, however, domestic concentration would be expected to have increased.

GOVERNMENTAL CONCENTRATION

Increased governmental concentration (or centralization) is one manifestation of increased domestic concentration. Concentration refers not to the absolute size and scope of a society's central government, but to its relative size. Generally, the resources mobilized in wartime increase the absolute size of government.[2] In addition, wartime mobilization increases the proportion of

TABLE 6-1
Average Annual Cost of American Wars in the Twentieth Century

War	Original Incremental Cost (billion $)	Duration (in months)	Average Annual Cost (billion $)	National Income in Prewar Year (billion $)	Average Annual Cost as % of National Income in Prewar Year
World War I	26.0	19	16.4	36.9	44
World War II	288.0	46	75.1	81.1	92.6
Korean War	54.0	37	17.5	217.5	8
Vietnam War	107.8	93	13.9	518.1	2.7

Sources: Tables 4-1 and 4-3.

TABLE 6-2
Comparison of Average Annual War Costs and Size of Federal Government Prior to the War

War	Average Annual Cost (billion $)	Total Federal Outlays in Prewar Year* (billion $)	Average Annual Cost as % of Federal Outlays	Federal Outlays for National Defense in Prewar Year* (billion $)	Average Annual Cost as % of Federal Outlays on Defense
World War I	16.4	.713	2300	.305	5377
World War II	75.1	9.589	783	1.504	4993
Korean War	17.5	40.570	43	13.097	134
Vietnam War	13.9	118.584	12	53.591	26

Sources: Table 6-1. U.S., Bureau of the Census, *Historical Statistics of the United States, Colonial Times to 1970* (Washington: Government Printing Office, 1976), pp. 1115–16, series Y466, Y467, Y472, Y473.
*Figures for prewar years are those for 1916, 1940, 1949, and 1964, respectively.

TABLE 6-3
Total Direct Federal Government Expenditures as Percent of GNP, 1902–74

Year	%	Year	%	Year	%
1902	2.6	1946	31.5	1962	18.9
1913	2.4	1948	13.1	1963	18.7
1918	17.0*	1950	14.9	1964	18.3
1919	22.3*	1952	20.0	1965	17.4
1922	4.9	1953	21.2	1966	17.3
1927	3.6	1954	20.5	1967	19.1
1932	7.0	1955	17.7	1968	19.3
1934	7.6	1956	17.3	1969	19.0
1936	10.0	1957	17.7	1970	18.9
1938	9.1	1958	18.2	1971	18.7
1940	9.2	1959	18.0	1972	17.8
1942	22.0	1960	17.9	1973	17.4
1944	47.3	1961	18.8	1974	18.0

Sources: U.S., Bureau of the Census, *Historical Statistics of the United States, Colonial Times to 1970* (Washington: Government Printing Office, 1976), p. 224, 1115, 1123–24, series F1, Y466, Y613. U.S., Bureau of the Census, *Statistical Abstract of the United States: 1973,* 94th ed. (1973), p. 416, table 665. U.S., Bureau of the Census, *Statistical Abstract of the United States: 1974,* 95th ed. (1974), p. 248, table 405. U.S., Bureau of the Census, *Statistical Abstract of the United States: 1975,* 96th ed. (1975), p. 255, table 421. U.S., Bureau of the Census, *Statistical Abstract of the United States: 1976,* 97th ed. (1976), pp. 261, 393, tables 425, 628.

*Figures for these years are based on estimates of federal expenditures. The estimates were created by taking the differences between data on federal expenditures and federal outlays for 1913 and 1922, interpolating difference figures for 1918 and 1919, and combining these interpolated differences with the actual federal outlays for those years.

authoritative decisions made by the central government relative to those of society's other governmental bodies.

Ascertaining the effect of wartime mobilization on the absolute size and scope of the federal government and its development is a relatively simple task. One way to do so is by looking at fluctuations of federal expenditures and employees, changes which indicate fluctuations in the number of tasks undertaken by government. The more decisions a government makes and the greater the scope of its activities, then the more employees are needed to carry out its policies and programs and the greater its expenditures are likely to be. Data on federal expenditures and employees are presented in table 6–3 and figures 6–1 and 6–2.[3]

All four American wars in the twentieth century have involved an increase in the scope of the federal sector. Federal expenditures in World War I reached one-fifth of the gross national product (GNP), whereas they were under 3 percent prior to the war. Federal civilian employees constituted twice the percentage of the civilian labor force in World War I than before it, growing from 1 percent prior to the war to over 2 percent during the war. Following the war, the federal sector receded in size, but remained larger than it was before the war.

The increase in the federal government's intervention in the economy and establishment of make-work programs during the depression of the 1930s is clearly evident in the data on federal employment. From a pre–World War I average of 1 percent of the total labor force, the percentage of federal employees grew during the war to an average of 2.1 percent, dropped back to an average of 1.2 percent in the years 1920–33, and then increased steadily through the period 1934–40 from 1.4 percent to 1.9 percent. Much the same pattern is revealed by the data on federal expenditures and purchases of goods and services.[4]

World War II brought a massive increase in the scope of the federal sector in the United States, even relative to the growth that had occurred during the depression years. During the war, federal expenditures reached almost one-half the entire GNP. The number of civilian employees also grew. After the war, the federal sector shrank, although it remained larger than it had been before the war; thus, this pattern is similar to the postwar trend of the early 1920s.

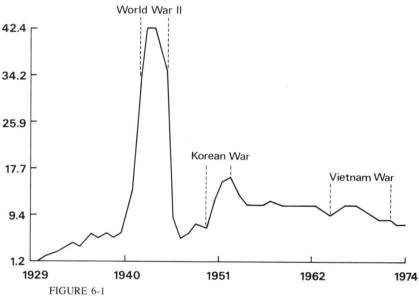

FIGURE 6-1
Federal Government Purchases of Goods and Services as Percent of GNP, 1929-74

Sources: U.S., Bureau of the Census, *Historical Statistics of the United States, Colonial Times to 1970* (Washington: Government Printing Office, 1976), p. 224, series F1. U.S., Department of Commerce, Office of Business Economics, *The National Income and Product Accounts of the United States, 1929-1965: Statistical Tables* (1965), pp. 52–53, table 3.1. U.S., Department of Commerce, Bureau of Economic Analysis, *The National Income and Product Accounts of the United States, 1929-1974: Statistical Tables* (1974), pp. 96–97, table 3.2. U.S., Bureau of the Census, *Statistical Abstract of the United States: 1976*, 97th ed. (1976), p. 393, table 628.

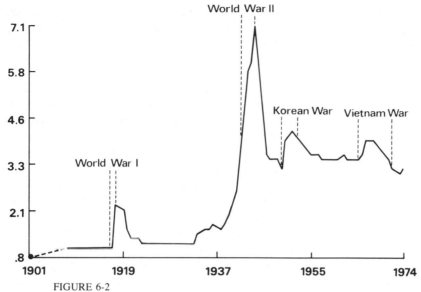

FIGURE 6-2

Civilian Employees of the Federal Government as Percent of Civilian Labor Force, 1901, 1908–74

Sources: U.S., Bureau of the Census, *Historical Statistics of the United States, Colonial Times to 1970* (Washington: Government Printing Office, 1976), pp. 126–27, 1102, series D4, D14, Y308. U.S., Bureau of the Census, *Statistical Abstract of the United States: 1974,* 95th ed. (1974), p. 236, table 389. U.S., Bureau of the Census, *Statistical Abstract of the United States: 1976,* 97th ed. (1976), pp. 249, 356, tables 409, 571.

The Korean War also brought an increase in the federal sector, although a much smaller one than those of the two previous wars. The war led to a modest increase in expenditures and purchases, although these were largely a function of the military mobilization alone. An analysis of federal civilian employment, which does not include the mobilized armed forces, shows that there was only a slight increase during the Korean War years. The pattern after the war was similar to those after the two world wars: the size of the federal government receded but remained larger than it had been before the war.

The Vietnam War involved an even smaller increase in the federal sector than did the Korean War. Given that the mobilization for this conflict was smaller than for any of the other three wars, it is not at all surprising that the increases in the federal sector during the period of the American involvement in Southeast Asia were slight. During the last years of the war, the federal sector actually began to recede, following the pattern that had emerged only after the three earlier wars had ended. This shrinkage in the size of the government coincided with the Vietnamization policy of the Nixon administration. Interestingly enough, the fragmentary evidence suggests that the post-Vietnam federal government was smaller in scope than it was prior to the war. This is quite different from the pattern following the other three wars, when the government contracted, although to a size larger than it had been before the war.

This pattern is called a ''displacement effect'' in the public finance literature, in which it is often claimed that public expenditures increase (relative to GNP and population) at times of crisis, especially wars.[5] The taxpayer's view of tolerable taxation is believed to increase as a function of the occurrence of a war or other major upheaval, such as a severe depression. After the end of the crisis, people expect that they will be required to contribute less. Yet the very existence of the crisis has served to increase their view of tolerable taxation, while the passage of time has dimmed the memory of the size of their prewar contribution. Thus, they are willing to support a larger government than existed prior to the war, although not as large as during the crisis itself. When a war is over, therefore, it is expected that nondefense expenditures will replace some, but not all, emergency expenditures. Governments do not spend as much (relative to GNP) as they did during war, but spend more than they did before it. War is thus a major determinant in the historical growth of the state.[6] A ''displacement effect'' accurately describes most of the American war experiences in the twentieth century. The Vietnam case, however, adds an interesting wrinkle to the argument; it suggests that war may not always have a positive ''displacement effect,'' but may cause ''negative displacement'' as well.

The relationship between mobilization and domestic cohesion provides an explanation for the negative displacement effect of the Vietnam War. War-time mobilization leads to a decrease in domestic cohesion independent of the ways in which war might be expected to have the opposite effect. This discord, a function of the nature of the good provided (a collective one) and the clarity of the link between costs and benefits in wartime, was particularly severe during the Vietnam War. At the same time, many of the resources expended for the war were not extracted for that specific purpose. Rather, the government diverted already extracted resources to the war effort. Thus, individuals came to see a clear link between the war and some of what had been their peacetime contribution to the costs of government. This, along with the relatively large increases in individual disaffection given the small extent of the mobilization, led to a particularly strong expectation that government expenditures would decrease after the war, relieving people of part of the burden they had carried even before the conflict began. Yet because of the low level of mobilization and the diversion of previously extracted resources for the war effort, the expected postwar decline in government spending could be met only if the government shrank to a size smaller than it was before the war.

Thus, the Vietnam War effected a "negative displacement" in the size of the government. Ironically, it is this decrease in the scope of governmental activity which constituted the "windfall" many expected to follow the end of the war. Rather than freeing up new resources for social welfare expenditures, the end of the war meant that a greater proportion of the national product was spent by individuals than by government.

Evidence of a displacement effect does not, however, confirm the hypothesis that war leads to increased governmental concentration, for such a change would be evinced by fluctuations in the size of the central government relative to other governmental units in the society. In the United States, therefore, increases in governmental centralization are indicated by increases in the ratio of the size of the federal government to state and local governments.[7] Such comparisons are presented in table 6-4 and figures 6-3 and 6-4.

Only twice during the twentieth century, during World Wars I and II, did federal nondefense expenditures exceed total state and local government expenditures in the United States. No such increase in governmental centralization occurred during the Korean and Vietnam Wars. The ratio of federal purchases of goods and services to state and local purchases of goods and services shows the same pattern for the period beginning in 1929. The ratio of federal civilian employees to state and local government employees reinforces the picture obtained in the analysis of relative expenditures. Only during World War II did the federal government employ more civilians than all state and local governments combined. A comparison of the number of federal employees during World War I with any reasonable estimate of the number of state and local employees during that time indicates that there was an increase in governmental centralization during World War I as well.[8] During the Korean War, centralization increased only slightly, and during the Vietnam War not at all.

This analysis confirms the expectations developed above. During both world wars, the United States undertook massive mobilizations and experienced increases in governmental centralization. The smaller mobilizations of the Korean and Vietnam Wars, efforts not expected to lead to increased centralization, did not in fact do so. The increased governmental centralization that occurred during the two world wars is reflected by the actions of the federal government as well as by the data on expenditures and employees. During the world wars, the federal government responded to the requisites of mobilization by expanding its role and instituting policies and programs unlike any it had previously or has since established. Examples include the rationing of consumer goods and direct allocation of scarce resources. Such changes in governmental behavior were simply not required during the smaller mobilizations of the Korean and Vietnam Wars.

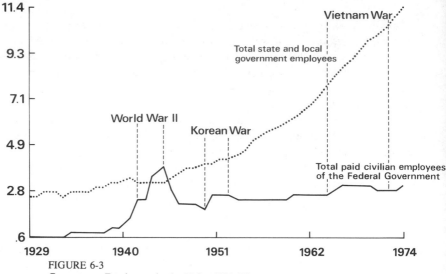

IN MILLIONS

FIGURE 6-3
Government Employees in the U.S., 1929–74

Sources: U.S., Bureau of the Census, *Historical Statistics of the United States, Colonial Times to 1970* (Washington: Government Printing Office, 1976), pp. 1102, 1104, series Y308, Y332. U.S., Bureau of the Census, *Statistical Abstract of the United States: 1974*, 95th ed. (1974), p. 236, table 389. U.S., Bureau of the Census, *Statistical Abstract of the United States: 1976*, 97th ed. (1976), p. 249, table 409. U.S., Bureau of Labor Statistics, *Employment and Earnings, United States, 1909–1975*, Bulletin 1312-10 (1976), p. 679.

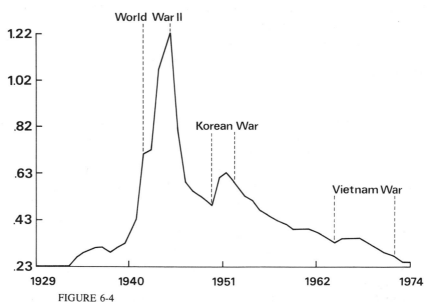

FIGURE 6-4
U.S. Governmental Concentration, 1929–74, Indicated by Ratio of Federal Civilian Employees to State and Local Government Employees

Source: Figure 6-3

62

TABLE 6-4
U.S. Government Concentration: Expenditures, 1902–73

	Ratio of Total Direct Expenditures to Total State and Local Government Expenditures				
Year	Total Federal Expenditures	Nondefense Federal Expenditures	Year	Total Federal Expenditures	Nondefense Federal Expenditures
1902	.52	.37	1955	1.74	.67
1913	.42	.31	1956	1.68	.68
1918*	3.13	1.43	1957	1.64	.64
1919*	4.15	1.17	1958	1.51	.63
1922	.64	.49	1959	1.49	.64
1927	.44	.36	1960	1.48	.68
1932	.48	.39	1961	1.46	.70
1934	.63	.56	1962	1.50	.72
1936	.97	.86	1963	1.48	.72
1938	.77	.67	1964	1.44	.73
1940	.82	.675	1965	1.37	.73
1942	3.18	.74	1966	1.37	.73
1944	9.47	1.33	1967	1.43	.73
1946	4.67	1.08	1968	1.43	.71
1948	1.59	.83	1969	1.34	.70
1950	1.52	.86	1970	1.25	.68
1952	2.24	.67	1971	1.16	.69
1953	2.34	.71	1972	1.10	.68
1954	2.04	.70	1973	1.11	.70

Sources: U.S., Bureau of the Census, *Historical Statistics of the United States, Colonial Times to 1970* (Washington: Government Printing Office, 1976), pp. 1115, 1123–24, 1127, series Y466, Y467, Y613, Y615, Y671. U.S., Bureau of the Census, *Statistical Abstract of the United States: 1973,* 94th ed. (1973), pp. 415–16, tables 663, 665. U.S., Bureau of the Census, *Statistical Abstract of the United States: 1974,* 95th ed. (1974), pp. 247–48, tables 403, 405. U.S., Bureau of the Census, *Statistical Abstract of the United States: 1975,* 96th ed. (1975), p. 255, table 421. U.S., Bureau of the Census, *Statistical Abstract of the United States: 1976,* 97th ed. (1976), pp. 260–61, tables 423, 425.

Note: The correlation between these two ratios is .76. The correlation between the ratio using all federal expenditures and that based on employees (figure 6-4) is .90. The correlation between the ratio using federal nondefense expenditures and that based on employees is .74.

*Based on estimates. The estimation procedure for the federal data is discussed in table 6-3. Figures for state and local expenditures for these years were estimated by interpolation.

POPULATION CONCENTRATION

Changes in population concentration occur when individuals move. If they migrate from areas that are highly populated to ones less populated, then the distribution of the population becomes more equal and concentration decreases. If the migration is from less highly populated areas toward more highly populated ones, the distribution of the population becomes more concentrated.

One typical pattern of migration in wartime is from rural areas to urban ones, for the manufacturing concerns that are predominantly located in urban areas are likely to require additional laborers in order to meet the demands of massive mobilization. Migration between rural and urban areas is a common

TABLE 6-5
Changes in U.S. Farm Population, 1910–70

Year	Change in Farm Population From Previous Year (in 1000s)	Year	Change in Farm Population From Previous Year (in 1000s)	Year	Change in Farm Population From Previous Year (in 1000s)
1911	+33	1931	+316	1951	−1158
1912	+100	1932	+543	1952	−142
1913	+60	1933	+1005	1953	−1874
1914	+50	1934	−88	1954	−855
1915	+120	1935	−144	1955	+59
1916	+90	1936	−424	1956	−366
1917	−100	1937	−471	1957	−1056
1918	−480	1938	−286	1958	−528
1919	−750	1939	−140	1959	−536
1920	+774	1940	−293	1960	−957
1921	+149	1941	−429	1961	−832
1922	−14	1942	−1204	1962	−490
1923	−619	1943	−2728	1963	−946
1924	−313	1944	−1371	1964	−413
1925	+13	1945	−395	1965	−591
1926	−211	1946	+983	1966	−768
1927	−449	1947	+426	1967	−720
1928	+18	1948	−1446	1968	−421
1929	+32	1949	−189	1969	−147
1930	−51	1950	−1146	1970	−595

Source: U.S., Department of Agriculture, Rural Development Service, *Farm Population Estimates, 1910–1970,* by Vera J. Banks and Calvin L. Beale, Statistical Bulletin 523 (July 1973), pp. 14–15, table 1.

phenomenon in industrializing societies. Thus any war-induced increase in population concentration in the United States would be in addition to the secular trend, for there has been a steady decline in the farm population of the United States during the twentieth century, as shown in table 6–5.[9] In 1910, more than 30 million Americans lived on farms and constituted more than one-third of the total population. By 1970, the farm population was less than 10 million and constituted less than 5 percent of the American population. There was, however, tremendous yearly variation in the overall secular decline of the farm population. The farm population was still growing between 1910 and 1916; decline did not begin until 1916/17. The first large exodus from American farms, in 1918 and 1919, occurred during the period of United States involvement in World War I. Immediately following the war, however, the farm population grew slightly for two years, and the next massive exodus from American farms was not until World War II. The American farm population, which had declined by only about 2 million people between 1910 and 1941, decreased by more than 5.5 million during the four years of World War II. The next large decline came during the Korean War, when the farm population dropped by more than 3 million. Thus, between 1910 and 1953,

TABLE 6-6
Percentage of U.S. Migrants, 1947–69

	Percentage of Migrants			Percentage of Migrants	
Year*	Between Counties†	Between States†	Year*	Between Counties†	Between States†
1947	6.4	3.1	1959	6.4	3.2
1948	5.8	3.0	1960	6.3	3.2
1949	5.6	2.6	1961	6.1	3.1
1950	7.1	3.5	1962	6.8	3.6
1951	6.6	3.4	1963	6.6	3.3
1952	6.6	3.6	1964	6.8	3.3
1953	6.4	3.2	1965	6.6	3.3
1954	6.6	3.1	1966	6.7	3.4
1955	6.8	3.1	1967	7.0	3.6
1956	6.2	3.1	1968	6.6	3.4
1957	6.7	3.3	1969	6.7	3.6
1958	6.1	3.0			

Source: U.S., Bureau of the Census, *Historical Statistics of the United States, Colonial Times to 1970* (Washington: Government Printing Office, 1976), p. 96, series C81, C85, C87.

*Surveys are taken in March or April and each year reference is to the period beginning in March or April and ending in March or April of the following year.

†Mobility status of the population one year old and over. Unfortunately, it does include some members of the armed forces.

the farm population decreased by more than 12 million people; slightly more than 9 million of these left during the first three American wars of the twentieth century. The secular decline in the farm population following the Korean War has continued apace without any marginal change during the Vietnam War.

Data on the total number of migrating Americans are not available for as long a period as are the data on the farm population. The United States Census Bureau only began to collect annual survey data after World War II, in part because they realized that their work had not adequately captured the massive migration of the war years. The data that are available show relatively little fluctuation in the percentage of Americans who moved across county or state lines. As expected, neither the Korean nor Vietnam Wars led to increased population movement in the United States.

There are no migration data at all for the era of World War I, but there is fragmentary evidence relevant to the American experience during World War II. In the period 1935–40, 13.1 percent of the population moved across county lines and 5.4 percent across state lines. For the period 1940–47, the comparable figures are 20.8 percent and 10.1 percent respectively.[10] Much of the latter migration occurred during the war years, and contemporaneous evidence suggests that there was, in fact, a massive wartime migration of the American population.

Changes in the amount of migration are not necessarily indicative of

TABLE 6-7
Net U.S. Interstate Migration Rate, 1870–1970

Time Period	Net Interstate Migration (percent of population)	Time Period	Net Interstate Migration (percent of population)
1870–1880	1.4*	1935–1940	1.1†
1880–1890	1.2*	1940–1950	3.7†
1890–1900	1.5*	1940–1943	2.6†
1900–1910	1.5*	1940–1946	3.4†
1910–1920	1.5*	1940–1947	3.5†
1920–1930	2.8*	1950–1960	3.4†
1930–1940	2.0*	1950–1951	.5†
		1950–1955	2.5†
		1955–1960	1.1†
		1960–1970	1.7†

Sources: U.S., Bureau of the Census, *Historical Statistics of the United States, Colonial Times to 1970* (Washington: Government Printing Office, 1976), p. 93, series C25–C75. U.S., Bureau of the Census, "Internal Migration in the United States, 1935–1940," *Population— Special Reports,* series P-44, no. 10 (April 7, 1944), p. 5, table 5. U.S., Bureau of the Census, "Interstate Migration and other Population Changes: 1940 to 1943," *Population—Special Reports,* series P-44, no. 17 (August 28, 1944), pp. 3–4. U.S., Bureau of the Census, "Estimated Population of the United States, by Regions, Divisions, and States: July 1, 1946," *Current Population Reports,* series P-25, no. 2 (August 15, 1947), p. 4, table 2. U.S., Bureau of the Census, "Estimates of the Population of the United States, by Regions, Divisions, and States: July 1, 1940 to 1947," *Current Population Reports,* series P-25, no. 12 (August 9, 1948), p. 6, table 2. U.S., Bureau of the Census, "Revised Estimates of the Population of States and Components of Population Change: 1950 to 1960," *Current Population Reports,* series P-25, no. 304 (April 8, 1965), pp. 13–14, table 4.

*Estimated using survival-rate method. Percent of resident population at beginning of decade.

†Estimated using components-of-change method. Percent of resident population at beginning of time period.

Net interstate migration represents the excess of out-migration over in-migration for the states that lost population through migration. This undoubtedly underestimates the gross number of interstate migrants.

changes in the distribution of population, however. The amount of migration need not lead to a redistribution of the population if the migrants cancel one another out. Table 6–7 provides data on net interstate migration, data that underestimate the total number of interstate migrants but represent the excess of out-migration over in-migration and thus provide a measure of the extent of population redistribution caused by the gross overall amount of migration. Estimates of net migration are generally not available on an annual basis, and are available only on a decennial basis prior to 1935, a period for which a weak estimation procedure further limits the usefulness of the data. The available data do not show any effect during the decade of World War I, and given that the war lasted for only nineteen months, it may be that poor data obscure changes that did, in fact, occur.[11]

The more accurate estimates of population redistribution available for the years since 1935 show clearly the impact of World War II. During the five years from 1935 to 1940, migration led to a net shift of 1.1 percent of the

American population. During the three years from 1940 to 1943, there was a net shift of 2.6 percent of the population. Illustrative evidence suggests that much of this change was related to the war effort. During the entire decade, 3.7 percent of the population shifted, the largest decennial shift to occur between 1940 and 1970. Most of the shift occurred in the first half of the decade as a result of the mobilization effort for World War II.

Despite the postwar mobility of the American people, the net population change since World War II has been relatively slight. Unlike the Korean and Vietnam Wars, which did not result in an unusual redistribution of the American population, World War II involved a relatively large redistribution of the American population in a very short period of time.

A net population shift does not, however, necessarily indicate a change in the concentration of the population, unless it affects densely populated areas. An evaluation of the effects of war on concentration thus requires an analysis of the changes in the relative proportion that live in certain areas. The number of Americans living in urban or metropolitan areas has grown in every decade of the twentieth century. The increases have been relatively equally distributed over time. They do not appear to be especially associated with war involvement, although aggregate decennial data may mask important yearly differences.

Population concentration calculated on the basis of regional divisions, on the other hand, shows very slight differences over the course of the century. The two largest states constituted 18 percent of the resident United States population in 1900 and 19 percent in 1970. The nine largest states contained 48 percent of the population in 1900 and 52 percent in 1970. Large migrations have not resulted in large changes in concentration because the migration has not been into highly populated states. Rather, the major internal American migration during the century has been to the Far West, one of the least populated areas of the country. In 1900, the two largest states were New York and Pennsylvania; in 1970, they were California and New York. Only 6 percent of population lived in the Western states in 1900; 17 percent lived there in 1970. Thus, the regional distribution of population has not evinced an increase in concentration during the century.

Thus, the available data suggest that none of the four American wars in the twentieth century led to an unusual increase in population concentration. Rather, the pattern of migration over the course of the century has been largely uniform. Although the pattern accords with expectations for the Korean and Vietnam Wars, it contradicts those for the world wars. This is especially true of World War II, for which the available illustrative evidence points not only to heavy migration but to increased concentration as well. Contemporary concern, in fact, led to the creation of a Select Committee Investigating National Defense Migration in the U.S. House of Representa-

TABLE 6-8
Percentage of U.S. Population in Urban and Metropolitan Areas, 1900–1970

	Percentage of Population	
Year	Urban Areas	Metropolitan Areas
1900	39.6	41.9
1910	45.6	45.7
1920	51.2	49.7
1930	56.1	54.3
1940	56.5	55.1
1950	64.0*	59.2
1960	69.9*	63.0
1970	73.5*	64.4

Source: U.S., Executive Office of the President: Office of Management and Budget, Social Indicators 1973 (Washington: Government Printing Office, 1973), p. 258, tables 8/12, 8/13.
*A different definition of urban is used for these figures. The percentage living in urban areas in 1950, calculated using the old definition of urban was 59.6.

tives. Similar concern was expressed by the executive branch, and the president established a Committee for Congested Production Areas. The Bureau of the Census devoted special attention to these areas. This concern was not unfounded, for certain regions were the targets of massive in-migrations during both world wars. Such population shifts are not, however, evidence of increased population concentration in the United States. The congested production areas of World War II were rarely established in already heavily populated areas. Thus, the shift to these areas did not increase the overall degree of concentration. Five of the ten congested production areas were on the West Coast, and the movement to these areas simply continued a trend that had begun earlier and has been sustained since. Three of the remaining five congested production areas were in the coastal Southeast, bringing migrants into a region from which many others were fleeing. Only two of the ten congested production areas were highly populated prior to the war. Thus, it appears that governments can independently affect one of the other manifestations of domestic concentration, the distribution of population.

INDUSTRIAL CONCENTRATION

It is also hypothesized in chapter 2 that wartime mobilization leads to an increase in a society's industrial concentration. Adequate measures of industrial concentration are not available for the entire century and are not fully comparable over time. Direct indication of changes in industrial concentration is available annually from 1931, however, when the Internal Revenue Service began to publish data on the number of returns by asset-size classes. Thus, it is possible to calculate the proportion of total corporate assets held by the largest firms in the society.[12] Table 6–9 provides these data. Clearly the

TABLE 6-9
Degree of U.S. Industrial Concentration, 1931–72

Percentage of Assets Held by Largest Corporations with Assets Greater than Zero			
Year	*Top .15%*	*Year*	*Top .1%*
1931	47.2	1954	48.6
1932	50.6	1955	50.0
1933	52.2	1956	50.1
1942	53.4	1957	50.9
1943	53.0	1958	51.3
1944	53.0	1959	51.9
1945	52.7	1960	52.6
1946	51.0	1961	53.2
1947	51.6	1962	53.3
1948	52.4	1963	53.8
1949	53.3	1964	54.3
1950	52.8	1965	54.9
1951	53.5	1966	55.7
1952	53.2	1967	57.3
1953	53.6	1968	58.1
1954	54.3	1969	59.0
1955	54.5	1970	60.6
		1971	61.7
		1972	62.0

Sources: U.S., Internal Revenue Service, *Statistics of Income, 1931–1972, Corporation Income Tax Returns* (Washington: Government Printing Office, 1933–77).
Note: The percentage of active corporations in the highest asset classes and the percentage of total assets they control were calculated from Internal Revenue Service data on the distribution of corporate returns and assets by total asset classes. The above figures were then derived by interpolation. The data for the period 1934–41 are not comparable with earlier or later years. A change in the tax law withdrew the privilege of filing consolidated returns. The most that can be inferred from the data for these years is that the degree of concentration probably increased during this period.

degree of industrial concentration has increased secularly since 1931, except during and immediately following World War II. Counter to expectations, therefore, World War II served to decrease rather than increase industrial concentration. The pattern for the Korean and Vietnam War years, however, is as predicted; these wars did not effect changes in industrial concentration.

It is also the case, however, that measuring changes in the degree of industrial concentration using IRS tax data on assets underestimates the increased concentration that occurred during World War II. This is because many large firms with massive assets were not included in the tax data since they were publicly owned. The American mobilization for World War II involved not only government purchases of goods and services from private business, but the movement of the federal government into the production process as well. Thus, almost half of the $33 billion spent on construction and facilities during the war (until 1944) was spent in the construction of war plants (as opposed to military installations). These plants were major additions to the nation's industrial base, but they are not included in the data on total assets of private corporate firms in the society. Further, these plants were large: nearly a third of the units exceeded $50 million, and nearly three-quarters exceeded $10 million. Thus, it appears that the mobilization did indeed increase American industrial concentration: "it was apparent that wartime requirements had resulted in markedly increasing the scale of big business."[13] It was certainly assumed during and immediately after the war that such concentration had taken place. President Truman, for example, remarked in his 1947 State of the Union message that "during this war this long-standing tendency toward economic concentration was accelerated,"[14] and the need to deal with this change in the nation's production process became a concern of public policy: "These developments carried the inference that the disparity between big business and the rest of the economic structure had been accentuated during the war to proportions endangering the competititve balance. Containment of the economic power vested in the large corporation was again given a place of major importance in public policy."[15]

Interestingly, the government's own war plants provided a means with which to change the degree of industrial concentration, and Congress passed the Surplus Property Act in 1944 to turn the plants over to new or small companies rather than to the big ones that had built and operated them for the government during the war. Prior to World War II, for example, ALCOA (the Aluminum Corporation of America) held a dominant position in the nation's aluminum industry. During the war, it built aluminum plants for the government. After the war, however, the government decided to sell or lease those facilities to two small companies, Kaiser and Reynolds, in order to deconcentrate the industry. Such governmental action was only possible in a few industries, but it was combined with litigation intended to force divestiture of holdings by large firms.[16] The aggregate data on concentration of assets reveals that the government's involvement in the production process and its policy of relinquishing its war plants and other surplus property in such a way as to decrease concentration worked; it achieved the only sustained decline in concentration in the United States since 1931.

Briefly then, the available evidence also confirms the expectation that the Korean and Vietnam Wars did not affect industrial concentration; the basic secular trend was unaffected by these two conflicts. There is no evidence of increased concentration during World War I, but the data are incomplete and do not actually disprove expectations. The total evidence suggests that there probably was an increase in overall industrial concentration (private and public sector production facilities) during World War II. Indeed, this war was different than the others for it involved the government's entry into the actual production of goods needed for the war effort. The experience of World War

II also reaffirms the importance of government policy as an independent determinant of changes in industrial concentration. When mobilization exceeds the critical threshold, increased governmental concentration is immediately and clearly evidenced. This increase in centralized governmental decision-making makes possible the attenuation of the other manifestations of increased concentration that would be expected to occur.

SUMMARY

The empirical evidence on wartime changes in domestic concentration affirms certain expectations but also suggests increased subtlety. As expected, the Korean and Vietnam Wars did not cause an increase in any of the manifestations of concentration. For World Wars I and II, the evidence is mixed. Both world wars clearly led to an increase in the degree of governmental concentration. The little available data on population concentration and industrial concentration during World War I do not support the expectation of increased concentration. It should be noted that the evidence is too fragmentary for firm conclusions to be reached, however. World War II, on the other hand, was accompanied by a mobilization-induced increase in concentration, although of a smaller magnitude than expected. Population changes were small relative to the size of the total population, and governmental policy served to attenuate the expected increases in concentration. The increase in governmental centralization during World War II was so great that the government could consciously establish policies intended to counteract the increased concentration that might normally have occurred.

7

PARTICIPATION, WELFARE, AND INEQUALITY

THIS CHAPTER tests the argument presented in chapter 3 that wartime mobilization decreases the inequality of the distribution of goods among the members of society via three separate links. The analysis here focuses on each of these links in turn, and is devoted mainly to the effects of war on income distribution, although it does note the effects of war on the distribution of other goods as well. The chapter concludes with a discussion of the cumulative effect of wartime mobilization on societal inequality.

MOBILIZATION, PARTICIPATION, AND INEQUALITY

One way in which inequality decreases during wartime is as a function of the increased number of productive social participants necessitated by mobilization. Briefly, the mobilization process generally requires growth in the size of the labor force since the economy operates at a higher capacity due to the demands of the war effort. In addition, it is necessary to replace those workers who leave the production process to enter the armed forces. The most immediately available source of additional workers is the ranks of the unemployed, and as wartime mobilization thus brings nonparticipants into the production process, these new workers obviously obtain more of the social product than they did before war began. Figure 7-1 presents the yearly percentage of unemployed individuals in the United States in the twentieth century, and shows clearly that fewer people are unemployed in wartime than in peacetime. In World War I, the unemployment rate dropped to a low of 1.4 percent. It then began to climb, however, growing immensely during the depression and reaching a high of 24.9 percent in 1933. In World War II, the rate dipped to a new century low of 1.2 percent. During the Korean War, the unemployment rate dropped to 2.9 percent, a point lower than in any peacetime year during the period 1927–72. In the Vietnam War years, unemployment fell to 3.5 percent, still lower than any peacetime year since 1930. Not surprisingly, the size of the drop in the unemployment rate that has accompanied each of the four American wars of the twentieth century has been in direct proportion to the scope of the mobilization (i.e., the drop is greatest in the war with the greatest mobilization, etc.). Such wartime decreases in unemployment are common. In Great Britain, for example, the unemployment rate reached a low of .4 percent in World War I and dropped to .5 percent in World War II.[1]

The movement of individuals from the status of nonparticipants to participants is especially significant for the minority members of a society. The wartime increase in the participation of nonwhites in American wars has been relatively greater than that of whites. The last to be employed in peacetime

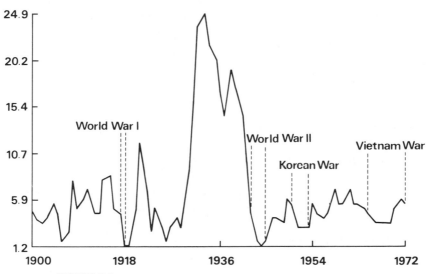

FIGURE 7-1
Percent of U.S. Civilian Labor Force Unemployed, 1900–1972

Sources: U.S., Bureau of the Census, *Historical Statistics of the United States, Colonial Times to 1970* (Washington: Government Printing Office, 1976), p. 135, series D85. U.S., Department of Labor, Bureau of Labor Statistics, *Handbook of Labor Statistics 1974*, BLS Bulletin 825 (1974), p. 27, table 1.

TABLE 7-1
U.S. Nonwhite Unemployment Rate, 1948–72

Year	Nonwhite Unemployment Rate*	Year	Nonwhite Unemployment Rate*	Year	Nonwhite Unemployment Rate*
1948	5.9	1957	7.9	1965	8.1
1949	8.9	1958	12.6	1966	7.3
1950	9.0	1959	10.7	1967	7.4
1951	5.3	1960	10.2	1968	6.7
1952	5.4	1961	12.4	1969	6.4
1953	4.5	1962	10.9	1970	8.2
1954	9.9	1963	10.8	1971	9.9
1955	8.7	1964	9.6	1972	10.0
1956	8.3				

Sources: U.S., Bureau of the Census, Historical Statistics of the United States, Colonial Times to 1970 (Washington: Government Printing Office, 1976), p. 135, series D93. U.S., Department of Labor, Bureau of Labor Statistics, Handbook of Labor Statistics 1974, BLS Bulletin 825 (1974), p. 143, table 59.
*Percent of persons sixteen years old and over in the labor force.

find doors suddenly opened to them during a wartime mobilization effort. The nonwhite unemployment rate is displayed in table 7-1. As with the overall unemployment rate, nonwhite unemployment dropped during the Korean and Vietnam Wars, due in part to increased nonwhite participation in the armed forces and in part to increased participation in the work force. Nonwhite unemployment reached a low of 4.5 percent in the Korean War and 6.4 percent during the Vietnam War. Again, the greater the mobilization effort, the greater the increase in participation in the work force; and again, the change in nonwhite participation has been relatively greater than the change in overall participation. The unemployment rate during the Korean War dropped 3 percentage points for the entire population and 4.5 percentage points for nonwhites. During the Vietnam War, unemployment dropped 1.7 percentage points for the total population and 3.2 percentage points for nonwhites.

When wartime mobilization is very large, those who join the labor force may include people who were not actively seeking work before the war. One example is the wartime participation of women in the labor force, as displayed in figure 7-2. The participation rate of women had been largely stable prior to World War II, but grew tremendously during the war itself, followed by a sharp postwar drop and a continuous secular increase since.

Individuals who are neither employed nor seeking employment are not officially considered to be members of the labor force. When the unemployment rate drops so low that a large number of such individuals do become productive participants, their move into the labor force is referred to as "negative unemployment."[2] During World War II, when the mobilization effort demanded a substantial increase in the size of the labor force, "negative unemployment'' occurred.[3] There were no increases in the participation of women which appear uniquely related to the occurrence of either the Korean or Vietnam Wars, and there was no evidence of negative unemployment in either war. Adequate data are not available for World War I, and there is some dispute as to whether that war produced negative unemployment.[4]

The available data clearly show that wartime mobilization leads to increases in the number of social participants. In wars that involve relatively small mobilization efforts, the new participants are people who were unemployed before the conflict. That is, they were nonworkers actively seeking employment. All four of the American wars in the twentieth century involved mobilization efforts sufficiently large to lead to a decrease in the unemployment rate. In wars involving large mobilizations, the increases in the number of productive social participants include individuals who did not desire to be part of the labor force before the war began. The American experience in World War II clearly fits this pattern.

It is argued in chapter 3 that participants obtain more of the social product

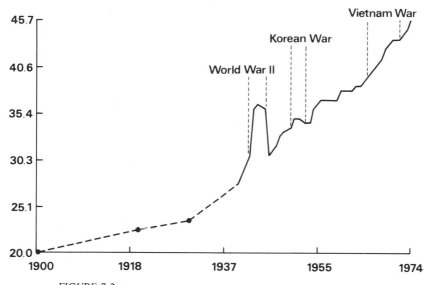

FIGURE 7-2
Female Participation Rate in the Labor Force, 1900, 1920, 1930, 1940–74, Shown by the Percentage of the Total Female Noninstitutional Population in the U.S. Labor Force

Sources: U.S., Bureau of the Census, *Historical Statistics of the United States, Colonial Times to 1970* (Washington: Government Printing Office, 1976), pp. 131–32, series D36. U.S., Department of Labor, Bureau of Labor Statistics, *Handbook of Labor Statistics 1974*, BLS Bulletin 825 (1974), p. 31, table 2. U.S., Department of Labor, Manpower Administration, *Manpower Report of the President* (April 1975), p. 205, table A-2.

than nonparticipants and that an increase in the number of participants thus leads to a decrease in inequality.[5] The available evidence does indeed support this contention. Empirical works on the macroeconomic determinants of changes in income inequality find strong direct relationships between the unemployment rate and measures of income inequality.[6] As the unemployment rate increases, so does the degree of income inequality. As the unemployment rate decreases, because more individuals participate in the work force and hold paying jobs, the degree of income inequality also decreases. The tightening of the labor market when unemployment is relatively low also leads to a narrowing of wage differentials, which also decreases the degree of income inequality.[7]

This relationship between participation and changes in inequality can be illustrated with regard to nonwhite Americans. Table 7–1 above shows that the nonwhite unemployment rate decreased during the Korean and Vietnam Wars. Figure 7–3 shows the changes in the ratio of the median income of nonwhite families to that of white families. That ratio increased during the Korean War and then dropped off, increased again during the mobilization phase of the Vietnam War, and then began to decrease during the Vietnamiza-

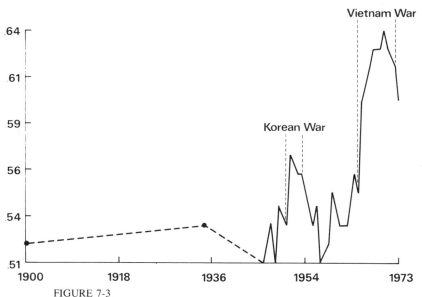

FIGURE 7-3
Ratio of Median Income of Nonwhite Families to White Families in the U.S., 1900, 1935, 1947–73

Sources: Stanley Lebergott, *The American Economy: Income, Wealth, and Want* (Princeton, N.J.: Princeton University Press, 1976), p. 301. U.S., Bureau of the Census, "Money Income in 1974 of Families and Persons in the United States," *Current Population Reports,* series P-60, no. 101 (January 1976), p. 24, table 13.

tion (demobilization) phase of the war. The correlation between the unemployment rate and the ratio of nonwhite to white family median income during the period 1948–72 is −.30.

The wartime changes in participation effect changes in the distribution of goods other than income as well. The increased participation of women during the two world wars, for example, also caused an increase in status returns to women.[8] Nor is it a coincidence that the political enfranchisement of women in Great Britain and the United States is correlated with the involvement of these nations in World War I.

EXTRACTION AND INEQUALITY

A second link between wartime mobilization and inequality is the manner in which distributed goods are extracted. The following empirical discussion deals with income, the most important of such goods. Governments extract income in two ways, taxes and inflation.[9] In the first case, income is extracted directly. During inflationary periods, however, governments typically extract the purchasing power of income by printing extra money. Both of these methods of extraction affect inequality, and both are generally employed in wartime.

War, independent of any taxation imposed to finance it, is usually accompanied by inflation, and it is widely accepted that inflation has a redistributive (equalizing) effect on the distribution of income.[10] Even when governments do not print extra money, they typically extract or divert production in the course of mobilization. As a result, shortages of desired items develop and the prices of these commodities become inflated. Inflation indeed grew in each of the four twentieth-century American wars, although not always at a faster rate than before the war. This is shown in the data on the consumer price index in figure 7–4. Thus, it can be assumed that these mobilization efforts served to decrease inequality by engendering wartime inflation.

Since inflation alone cannot finance most wars, however, taxation is also necessary, and governments place greater reliance on progressive taxes than on other means of raising revenues during wartime. Thus, it is to be expected that the proportion of government revenue raised via income taxes, the most progressive of taxes,[11] would increase in wartime. Table 7–2 presents the proportion of all governmental revenues in the United States constituted by individual and corporate income taxes and the proportion of federal revenues made up by these taxes. The most obvious feature of this data is that there was greater reliance on progressive taxes during World War II than at any time prior to or since the war. In 1940, income taxes provided 14 percent of all governmental revenues and 30 percent of federal revenues; by 1944, income taxes accounted for 54 percent of all governmental revenues and 74 percent of federal revenues. The only time since World War II that income taxes have provided more than half of all governmental revenues was during the Korean War, when they contributed 51 percent.

The proportion of government revenues contributed by income taxes reequilibrated following World War II at a level lower than the wartime peak but higher than the prewar level. The contribution of the income tax increased again during the Korean War and showed a similar postwar equilibration afterwards. The American involvement in Vietnam, however, did not effect any increase in the proportion of revenues contributed by income taxes. The government enacted no war-revenue measures early in the conflict, although it raised the telephone tax from 3 percent to 10 percent in 1966 in order to defray some of the costs of mobilization. The telephone tax is a regressive indirect tax, however, and the Vietnam experience is thus different from the three previous twentieth-century wars, when special revenue measures, including increasing the progressive income tax, were established immediately upon entry into the war. Yet even for the smaller mobilization of the Vietnam War, it finally became necessary to increase taxes, although the government was unwilling to do so in an obvious fashion. Thus, a surcharge on the federal income tax was finally enacted in 1968. The effect of this action can be seen

FIGURE 7-4
U.S. Consumer Price Index, 1900–1973 (1967 = 100)

Sources: U.S., Bureau of the Census, *Historical Statistics of the United States, Colonial Times to 1970* (Washington: Government Printing Office, 1976), pp. 210–11, series E135. U.S., President, *Economic Report of the President* (February 1974), p. 300.

TABLE 7-2
U.S. Degree of Reliance on Progressive Taxation, 1922–70

	Proportion of Revenues Raised via Individual and Corporate Income Taxes				
Year	All Government Revenues	Federal Revenues	Year	All Government Revenues	Federal Revenues
1922	.22		1953	.51	.71
1927	.19		1954	.49	.73
1932	.11		1955	.46	.71
1934	.08		1956	.46	.71
1936	.12		1957	.46	.71
1938	.17		1958	.44	.69
1940	.14	.30	1959	.43	.68
1941		.37	1960	.43	.67
1942	.30	.53	1961	.42	.66
1943		.64	1962	.42	.66
1944	.54	.74	1963	.41	.65
1945		.69	1964	.40	.64
1946	.47	.65	1965	.40	.64
1947		.61	1966	.41	.65
1948	.45	.64	1967	.41	.64
1949		.64	1968	.40	.63
1950	.41	.64	1969	.44	.66
1951		.67	1970	.41	.64
1952	.51	.72			

Source: U.S., Bureau of the Census, *Historical Statistics of the United States, Colonial Times to 1970* (Washington: Government Printing Office, 1976), pp. 1105, 1119, series Y343, Y345, Y346, Y505, Y508, Y509.

in the observation for 1969, when the proportion of revenues contributed by income taxes increased for the first time during the war.

The evidence available for World War I also confirms that the government increased its reliance on progressive income taxes during that conflict. The new federal income tax was at first levied on a minority of Americans. In 1916, only those with incomes exceeding $3,000 a year had to file returns, and fewer than half a million were in fact filed. In 1917, however, the enactment of a special War Revenue Act required individuals earning more than $1,000 a year to file returns, and those with incomes exceeding $2,000 to pay taxes. Just under 3.5 million returns were filed. In addition, the taxes paid in 1917 included a war excess-profts tax. In all, income taxes immediately paid for 35 percent of the cost of World War I.

One way to assess the combined effect of increased wartime participation and increased wartime reliance on progressive taxation on inequality is to analyze the proportion of personal income going to wages and salaries, which together constitute the largest part of the income earned by lower and middle income groups in the United States. Other forms of income, such as dividends, interest, and earnings derived from the ownership of property, are disproportionately earned by those with higher overall incomes. In other words, wages and salaries are more equally distributed than other forms of personal income.[12] One of the main arguments here is that increased wartime participation leads to lessened inequality because more individuals become productive social participants and thus increase their earnings and because workers generally earn higher pay during wars as a result of the increased demand for labor. An increase in the share of personal income disbursed via wages and salaries during wartime would provide strong evidence for this hypothesis. It would also support the contention that mobilization brings about redistribution directly. The proportion of the personal income disbursed through wages and salaries is presented in figure 7–5.

In all four twentieth-century American wars there have been increases in the proportion of personal income constituted by wage and salary disbursements and other payments for human labor. The data for World War I, which are of poor quality, show an unexpected decrease in this proportion between 1916 and 1917 and then show a sharp increase in 1918.[13] The better data

FIGURE 7-5
Proportion of Personal Income Earned by Human Labor in the U.S., 1909–18, 1929–74

Sources: Daniel Creamer, *Personal Income During Business Cycles* (Princeton, N.J.: Princeton University Press, 1956), p. 120. U.S., Department of Commerce, Bureau of Economic Analysis, *The National Income and Product Accounts of the United States, 1929–1974: Statistical Tables* (Washington: Government Printing Office, 1974), pp. 66–67, 334.

available for the years following 1929 show a very clear pattern, however. Between 1935 and 1940, when the United States was slowly recovering from the depression, there was an increase from 61.7 percent to 64.9 percent in the proportion of income paid as reimbursement for human labor (hereafter referred to as labor income). During World War II, there was a large increase in the percentage of labor income, which reached a high of 72.1 percent in 1944, and during the postwar years the percentage dropped to a level higher than it was prior to the war. There was also an increase during the Korean War, with a labor income high of 71.5 pcercent in 1953. Once again, there was a postwar decline to a level higher than before the war. Here too, Vietnam shows a pattern different from that of the other three wars. During its mobilization phase, there was an increase in the proportion of personal income constituted by reimbursement for labor from 70.7 percent in 1965 to 72.8 percent in 1969. During the period of Vietnamization, on the other hand, the pattern was reversed: the percentage of labor income dropped steadily. Since labor income is more equally distributed than other forms of income, the wartime increases in the proportion of labor income represent an indirect measure of the decrease in inequality effected by mobilization.[14]

MOBILIZATION, SOCIAL SERVICES, AND INEQUALITY

The third and final causal link between wartime mobilization and changes in domestic inequality involves social services, for wartime mobilization may either increase or decrease their provision and thus effect changes in inequality. Empirical studies have shown that social service expenditures are redistributive and therefore serve to decrease inequality.[15]

Apparently, however, war has not affected federal social welfare expenditures. These expenditures, including veterans benefits (as displayed in figure 7–6), have grown exponentially since the 1930s and have maintained the same steady climb both during and between wars. Data on all federal social welfare expenditures excluding veterans payments show the same pattern (correlation between the two equals .9996). To conclude that the American involvement in the three latter twentieth-century wars did not affect the level of federal social welfare expenditures may not be fully accurate, however. It may be, for example, that expenditures for social services do increase but that the increase is not apparent in this aggregate data since other fixed expenditures, such as unemployment payments, decrease in wartime, leaving the overall level unchanged. Nonetheless, because the available data for the United States show no change in the level of federal social welfare expenditures related to the occurrence of war, it must be assumed that war has not, in fact, effected changes in inequality by increasing the aggregate provision of social services in the United States since 1929.[16]

WAR AND AMERICAN INEQUALITY

Despite war's apparent lack of effect on social services, it is still expected that the net effect of a nation's involvement in war is to decrease inequality. Ironically, some of the best evidence on the effects of war on American income inequality during World War I comes from data provided by the income tax newly instituted during that conflict.[17] This evidence is limited, however, in that a majority of Americans were not then required to file returns. As a result, the returns from those first years of federal income taxation cannot be used as a basis for inferences about the entire income distribution but are indicative only of the income patterns of upper-income Americans. The data available from the tax returns can be analyzed in a variety of ways, all of which suggest that income inequality increased during the initial years of World War I, when the United States was involved only as a supplier of European belligerents. Income inequality decreased, however, when the United States entered the war. That decrease was sustained into the immediate postwar years, but was followed by an increase in inequality during the 1920s. The percentage of income going to the top 1 percent of income

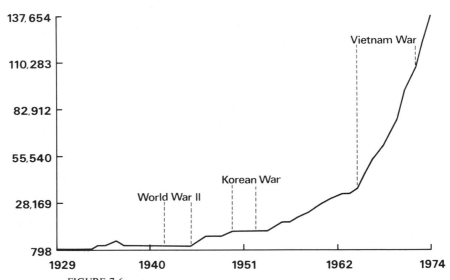

FIGURE 7-6
Federal Social Welfare Expenditures, 1929-74(in millions of $)

Sources: U.S., Bureau of the Census, Historical Statistics of the United States, Colonial Times to 1970 (Washington: Government Printing Office, 1976), p. 341, series H32. Alfred M. Skolnik and Sophie R. Dales, "Social Welfare Expenditures, 1950-75," Social Security Bulletin 39 (January 1976): 7. Alfred M. Skolnik and Sophie R. Dales, "Social Welfare Expenditures, 1972-73," Social Security Bulletin 37 (January 1974): 6.

TABLE 7-3
U.S. Income Inequality, 1913–19

Year	Inverse Pareto Slope	Percent of Income Received by Top 1%	Gini Inequality Measure
1913	.64		
1914	.65	13.07	
1915	.71	14.32	
1916	.74	15.58	.60033
1917	.68	14.16	.51032
1918	.61	12.69	.42938
1919	.60	12.96	.44437

Sources: Lee C. Soltow, "Evidence on Income Inequality in the United States, 1866–1965," *Journal of Economic History* 29 (June 1969): 282. U.S., Bureau of the Census, *Historical Statistics of the United States, Colonial Times to 1970* (Washington: Government Printing Office, 1976), p. 302, series G337. U.S., Internal Revenue Service, *Statistics of Income, 1916–19,* (Washington: Government Printing Office, 1919–22). Gini measure calculated by a computer program written by David Seidman, adapted by Donna Lustgarten, and modified by John Dingwall.

recipients, for example, increased by 2.5 points between 1914 and 1916 and then decreased by almost 3 points in the two war years, before increasing slightly in the immediate postwar years.

A study by Rufus S. Tucker, broader in that it incorporates data on all Americans earning more than $5,000 per annum and employs a half-dozen measures of inequality, confirms this pattern, however, except that it suggests that the decrease in inequality continued into the immediate postwar years: "All four methods of analysis and all three definitions of income agree that income was more concentrated before the War than immediately after; that concentration increased until 1928 or 1929 but did not reach its prewar intensity; and that concentration decreased until 1932 or 1933."[18] Briefly, this study concludes that "the War did not increase the concentration of income in the United States, but greatly diminished it."[19]

Lee C. Soltow's study using all the available information on taxable incomes, including those below $5,000, confirms these results. Table 7–3 also provides the inverse Pareto slope, one measure of inequality, for the years 1913–20.[20] The degree of inequality increased between 1913 and 1916 and dropped markedly in 1917 and 1918, to below the level of 1913. This decrease was sustained into 1919. An analysis using the Gini inequality measure as calculated from all the available returns (also presented in table 7–3) does not show the decrease in inequality to be sustained into 1919.[21]

The degree of inequality in the American distribution of income decreased during the 1920s. A variety of inequality measures (Pareto slopes, the share going to the top 1 percent, and the share going to the top 5 percent) all show such an increase. The conventional wisdom in the study of the American distribution of income is that inequality decreased in the period 1929–46. The

TABLE 7-4
U.S. Income Inequality, 1935–50

Year	Gini Inequality Measure
1935/36	.472
1941	.449
1944	.406
1946	.407
1947	.406
1950	.405

Source: Selma F. Goldsmith, George Jaszi, Hyman Kaitz, and Maurice Liebenberg, "Size Distribution of Income Since the Mid-Thirties," Review of Economics and Statistics 36 (February 1954): 7. Different authors use different ways of making the surveys comparable, and the use of different algorithms leads to some differences in the calculated measure. The differences are on the order of .01 and the pattern is the same. See Selma F. Goldsmith, "Statistical Information on the Distribution of Income by Size in the United States," American Economic Review 40 (May 1950): 330; Irving B. Kravis, The Structure of Income: Some Quantitative Essays (Philadelphia: University of Pennsylvania, Wharton School of Finance and Commerce, 1962), p. 204: Edward C. Budd, ed., Inequality and Poverty: An Introduction to a Current Issue of Public Policy (New York: W. W. Norton and Company, 1967), p. xiii.

percentage of income going to the top 1 percent of the income-receiving population clearly evinces a secular decrease. More specifically, this pattern would be expected to hold especially during the depression years. Yet one analysis focusing specifically on that period suggests that the cumulative effect of the depression was to increase the degree of inequality.[22] The losses to the poor and the massive growth in the unemployment rate more than offset the losses incurred by the rich and left inequality in American society greater than before. Others disagree, however, and conclude that inequality decreased between 1929 and 1933.[23] Despite the dispute over the pattern of the depression years, there is no disagreement about the nature of the changes that occurred during the period of slight recovery in the late 1930s or about the effects of World War II.

The inequality of income distribution in the United States decreased markedly during World War II. The data available for making such an assertion are much better than those for World World I. Extensive surveys of the distribution of American income were taken in both 1935/36 and 1941. Beginning in 1944, the American government undertook regular surveys of the American distribution of income, and the data from these sources are not limited to the upper part of the income distribution.[24] The Gini measure of inequality of American incomes is displayed in table 7–4.[25] Inequality markedly decreased during the late 1930s, as shown by a 5 percent decrease in the Gini measure for that six-year period. During the first three years of American involvement in World War II, the Gini measure dropped 10 percent. The degree of inequality then stabilized at the level it reached at the end of the war.[26] The major decrease in the degree of inequality in the United States during the war

TABLE 7-5
U.S. Income Inequality, 1944–71

Year	Gini Inequality Measure*	Redundancy Measure of Inequality†	Year	Gini Inequality Measure*	Redundancy Measure of Inequality†
1944	.436		1959	.422	.217
1945	.411		1960	.423	.218
1947	.430		1961	.432	.222
1948	.424		1962	.421	.216
1949	.428		1963	.418	.215
1950	.431		1964	.419	.210
1951	.416		1965	.417	.206
1952	.416		1966	.413	.197
1954	.429	.227	1967	.416	.195
1955	.420	.220	1968	.406	.186
1956	.415	.215	1969		.182
1957	.418	.210	1970		.188
1958	.416	.217	1971		.190

Sources: Edward C. Budd, "Postwar Changes in the Size Distribution of Income in the U.S.," *American Economic Review* 60 (May 1970): 255. Ann R. Horowitz, "Trends in the Distribution of Family Income within and between Racial Groups," in *Patterns of Racial Discrimination,* vol. 2: *Employment and Income,* ed. George M. von Furstenberg, Ann R. Horowitz, and Bennett Harrison (Lexington, Mass.: D. C. Heath and Company, 1974), p. 202.

*Families and Unrelated Individuals.
†Families.
Note: The correlation between the two measures for the years 1954–68 is .82.

is generally attributed to the increase in the share of personal income paid in return for human labor and to a reduction in wage differentials during the war.[27] As pointed out above, the increase in the participation rate in the labor force and the effects of taxation also played a role.[28] Indeed, "The war-time tax rates ... exerted a considerably more leveling effect than was felt in prewar years. For the upper segment of incomes, it appears that the 1942 tax structure was almost twice as effective in reducing the inequality of incomes as the tax structure in 1929."[29]

The conventional wisdom holding that the American distribution of income has remained unchanged during the postwar period[30] derives from the fact that there were apparently no continuous secular changes in the degree of inequality but only minor fluctuations during this period. Yet the Korean and Vietnam Wars may have effected changes in the degree of inequality. The foregoing analysis of the determinants of income inequality and indirect indications of changes in inequality would suggest such an effect. Any changes that did occur would not be as large as those evidenced during the world wars, however, since the two later mobilizations were not as large as those undertaken during the earlier wars. Table 7–5 presents the Gini measure of inequality for much of the postwar period, which shows slight decreases in inequality during both the Korean and Vietnam Wars.[31] Another measure of inequality, the redundancy measure, is also presented in table 7–5 for the years 1954–71.[32] This index shows that the decrease in inequality occasioned by the Vietnam War was sustained only until 1969, when inequality began to increase again. Again, the patterns for the mobilization and the Vietnamization periods of the conflict are different.

SUMMARY

The analysis here confirms that two of the three hypothesized causal links between wartime mobilization and changes in domestic inequality, the direct connection and the link to participation, served to decrease inequality during the four American twentieth-century wars. The link between mobilization and the provision of social services did not exist, however. Nonetheless, it is clear that inequality decreases in wartime and decreases most in wars with extensive mobilizations.

CONCLUSION: CONFLICT, MOBILIZATION, AND CHANGE

WARS ARE major determinants of change; they affect all aspects of a nation's domestic life and transform polity, society, and economy. Although political leaders rarely wage war for internal reasons, domestic ramifications are important, and should be considered as part of the decision to go to war. At the very least, knowledge of war's effects should guide decisions about the mobilization process, for war alters critical facets of domestic life. At the extreme, war can simultaneously rend the national fabric, shift the balance of governmental power, and narrow the gap between richer and poorer.

Common sense has war both increasing and decreasing domestic cohesion, and indeed war *can* increase national unity. Wars deemed necessary to the national interest by the political elite, but in which the population perceives no threat to the existence of the nation, will not increase cohesion. Cohesion increases at war's outset only when there exists a threat to the society; without threat, cohesion will never increase. The existence of an external threat is the necessary intervening variable that transforms war into a unifying force. Thus, political leaders who count on foreign adventures to unify their countries and cement their positions should think again. Manufacturing crises may enable leaders to expand the powers of the state but, in one manifestation or another, cohesion will surely decrease. Only if there is a perceived threat will cohesion increase.

87

Once a war has begun, however, the process of waging it always decreases cohesion. Every war, therefore, threatening or not, carries the costs of decreased cohesion. Because the level of cohesion decreases as a direct result of wartime mobilization, it drops immediately at war's outset when there is no threat, continues to decline throughout the course of the war, and will always be lower at the war's end than it was immediately before the war. A threatening war, on the other hand, is marked by an initial increase in cohesion, decreasing only as mobilization gets underway. The net change in domestic cohesion during a threatening war thus depends on both the existence of threat and the level of mobilization. If the threat is great, the mobilization small, and the time short, postwar cohesion will exceed prewar cohesion. In each of the cases examined here, however, the initial increase in cohesion at war's onset was followed by decreases in cohesion induced by the mobilization process, and the level of domestic cohesion was lower at each war's end then it was before the war.

Although wartime mobilization always fractures national unity, it does so differently in threatening wars than in nonthreatening and unpopular ones. Cohesion decreases because an increasing number of individuals balk at making personal sacrifices. Even in times of threat, people are reluctant to contribute to the provision of a collective good, one that each of them would presumably enjoy anyway. Nonetheless, such threatening wars are understood and accepted, and the marginal decreases in cohesion per unit of mobilization are smaller in threatening wars than in nonthreatening ones. Wars that demand sacrifice without the justification of threat put an even greater strain on national unity, for there is not even the acknowledgement that a public good is provided. Thus, the same levels of mobilization will lead to greater decreases in cohesion than when danger is believed to exist.

This suggests that real difference between the American experiences during World War II and Vietnam. The conventional wisdom is that cohesion increased in World War II but decreased during Vietnam. Indeed, today's politicians sometimes look longingly at the marvelous war effort of the early 1940s, a national project that seemed to pull the society together. Such historical images lead them to dub various contemporary undertakings ''wars,'' hoping to encourage individual sacrifices in ''moral equivalents of war.'' But their analogies are incorrect, for the massive mobilization of World War II, despite the pooling of individual effort, led nonetheless to a decrease in cohesion as a very direct result of those personal sacrifices. Of course, the existence of a threat did lead to an increase in cohesion during the initial stages of the war, and more important, the impact of mobilization on cohesion was limited by the existence of threat. It is this that makes the American experience in World War II unique among the cases studied here. Mobilization cannot be undertaken without decreasing cohesion, but the lesson of

World War II is that waging war can be accompanied by only slight decreases in cohesion.

By comparison, the domestic tragedy of Vietnam was dual. Absent a perceived threat, there was no initial increase in cohesion. More importantly, the relatively small mobilization led to large decreases in cohesion. To an unthreatened people, even slight sacrifices are intolerable. Moreover, given the lack of threat, the manifestations of decreased cohesion during Vietnam included political disapproval and dissent. Going to war when threatened is far more likely to be considered an important and appropriate action than doing so in times of relative safety, and thus threatening wars are more typically popular wars. The political disagreements that arise during them are limited to issues of strategy and tactics, and basic questions about the war's necessity and morality are left unasked. Thus, the decrease in cohesion in World War II was not manifested by political dissent, for a threat existed and the members of the society believed the state to be providing the security that they desired.

An unthreatening war, on the other hand, is by its very nature likely to be an unpopular one. The greater ambiguity of state activity means that the activity will be less accepted, and the war will be accompanied by the political manifestations of decreased cohesion. Charges of impropriety, luxury, and immorality are rarely heard from a threatened people, but they abounded during the period of United States involvement in Vietnam. Decreased cohesion included political protest against the government, and the most basic questions of importance and propriety were voiced and voiced often. For the level of mobilization, the decreases in cohesion were enormous. This is the lesson of Vietnam.

Only the state can wage war, for only it can mobilize and expend the resources required for battle and coordinate an entire society's military effort. Yet war may require changes in the way a society is organized for production. Not surprisingly, these changes are most visible in the political sector. In other words, war transforms polity as well as society, affecting both the size and scope of the state.

The most important of such changes are in the absolute size of the state itself. As the burdens of war increase governmental expenditures, the state acquires new capital by raising old taxes and creating new ones. In a threatening war, when the good provided is clear, the state typically raises funds through direct taxation. In a nonthreatening war, however, policy-makers tend to rely on less visible means of generating revenues; most typically, they depend on indirect taxation and inflation. In either case, however, the state grows, and the larger the mobilization the greater the growth.

Once the state has grown during wartime, it never returns to its prewar size. Once created, taxes do not disappear, for taxpayers get at least partly inured to paying them. As the adage suggests, "an old tax is a good tax," and the very taxes that were one determinant of decreased cohesion when they were first imposed seem less burdensome with the passage of time. They are never fully accepted, of course, and taxpayers do expect their burdens to be eased at war's end. Some taxes do in fact disappear, and others are lowered. But the decrease in state revenues is never as great as the wartime increase it follows. There is, in other words, a positive "displacement effect": war's end brings a reequilibration of revenues to a plateau higher than before the war.

To produce such a displacement, however, the state must newly extract the resources required for waging the war. Yet, if the state is large enough, and the war small enough, political leaders can instead choose to divert already extracted resources to the war effort. During Vietnam, for example, American leaders did not newly extract most of the resources needed for the war. Given the war's unpopularity, a function of its nonthreatening nature, they delayed raising taxes and refused to call up the reserves. This partial mobilization did not spare the society the full brunt of decreased cohesion, although those decreases would have been greater had mobilization been larger. The slight wartime mobilization did, however, alter the pattern of state growth and reequilibration. Even when most resources required for war are not specifically mobilized for the war effort, people still expect their wartime sacrifices to let up at war's end, even when those taxes are "old" ones. Thus, the end of war leads to a drop in the size of the state to below its prewar level. Again, the drop is not as great as the full costs of the war effort, but it does occur, and this "negative displacement effect" is the political cost borne of less than full mobilization, exacted when political leaders do not fully mobilize to fight a nonthreatening war. What the leaders save the society in decreased cohesion, they cost the political establishment in size and scope.

A war-induced displacement effect, whether positive or negative, is not the only political consequence of war. The displacement effect involves the relative proportion of national product consumed by the state, but war affects the state's scope as well, and can transform the nature of state activities as well as state size. When wartime mobilization (regardless of whether it diverts or newly extracts the required resources) is small relative to peacetime extraction, then mobilization does not change the state's role. When the mobilization is large relative to prewar extraction, however, then the state will not only be larger in size but also in scope as political centralization and concentration increase. The central state expands the scope of its activities to include ones previously within the domain of state and local governments, as well as those new to government altogether. The American mobilizations of the Korean and Vietnam Wars were not large enough to lead to changes in the degree of domestic concentration. During the world wars, however, extraction was much greater and did lead to an increase in government concentration.

As hypothesized in chapter 2, large-scale mobilization would seem to require not only increased centralization of government but the concentration of other factors of production (e.g., industry and population) as well. Yet only political concentration occurred during World War II. Despite the massize mobilization undertaken by the United States in the 1940s, these other aspects of production were unaffected. Ironically, it was the very increase in the scope of government that kept them unchanged, for newly expanded powers allowed policy-makers to establish programs intended to mitigate the expected increases in population and industrial concentration. As a monopoly organization, in other words, the state can control the degree of concentration in societal production, and the growth of state activity in wartime can encompass countervailing actions intended to prevent increased concentration in other aspects of the production process.

War also affects the distribution of goods among the members of the society, narrowing gaps in personal income and status. Of the three links between war and inequality hypothesized in chapter 3, two in fact exist. The direct link between mobilization and distribution, as well as that joining mobilization and distribution via participation, both hold.

As expected, wartime extraction is more progressive than peacetime extraction. The state, for example, generally increases its reliance on direct taxation—a typically progressive means of generating revenue. Even in a nonthreatening war, however, when political leaders often prefer to avoid such highly visible direct taxes, inequality diminishes. For inflation, which policy-makers tend to rely on to finance unpopular wars, is also progressive and redistributive. By either or both routes, therefore, war leads to greater income equality as a direct function of mobilization.

Wartime mobilization also reduces inequality indirectly by increasing the participation of individuals in societal production. The unemployed are drawn into the work force and unemployment rates reach all-time lows in wartime. When mobilization is large, even those not actively job hunting, and thus not counted among the unemployed, are drawn into the work force. Periods of war have for this reason been watersheds in the incorporation of women and minorities into active remunerative participation in the society's production process. Such increases in participation reduce the inequality in the distribution between rich and poor, for participants receive more income and status than nonparticipants.

War can also affect the governmental provision of funds for social welfare programs, programs that serve to reduce inequality through direct redistribution, among other means. There are, however, two plausible arguments detailing war's impact on social welfare appropriations. One is that wartime military expenditures replace those for social programs, thus serving to increase inequality. The other is that war actually promotes social spending by stimulating state concern with public well-being at precisely the time when it controls the resources to act on that concern. In this way, war would once again act to decrease inequality.

Yet, the evidence bears out neither of these contradictory propositions. In World War II, for example, the full military requirements of the United States were newly extracted. Despite this massive mobilization, however, which put vast resources into policy-makers' hands, social welfare expenditures did not significantly increase. During Vietnam, on the other hand, a war in which most war-required resources were diverted from peacetime purposes, there occurred no significant curtailment of social welfare programs. Funds came from peacetime military programs instead. In other words, the exponential growth of American social welfare expenditures during the course of the twentieth century was basically unaffected during wartime. Although such expenditures may well decrease inequality, they are clearly not a link through which war affects distribution—one way or the other.

The net effect of war, therefore, is to decrease the inequality in the distribution of goods, especially personal income and status, among the members of society. The gap in income between blacks and whites, and between rich and poor, has decreased in each American war in proportion to the mobilization. This relationship suggests another aspect of war-induced changes in the size and scope of the state. During wartime, the consumption of public goods increases relative to the consumption of private goods as a result of the increased proportion of national product controlled by the state, which primarily produces, and is the primary producer of, public goods. Thus, a shift in the balance between the public and private sectors is mirrored in a shift in the relative consumption of public and private goods. Because public goods are characterized by nonexcludability, such a shift reduces societal inequality.

Although the main focus of this study is on domestic effects of war during wartime itself, the empirical findings do extend to the immediate postwar periods and suggest that there exist striking similarities in the patterns of cohesion, concentration, and inequality during demobilization and immediately thereafter. The single most important finding is that, although the degree of change experienced in wartime may not be sustained, the changes caused by wartime mobilization become, to some extent, permanently ingrained. Although postwar mobilization does bring some reequilibration, there is never a return to the prewar level of cohesion or to the degrees of concentration and inequality. Nor is there a drop to the level that would be predicted by extrapolating from the prewar trend. The domestic effects of war are never reversed, and society does not return to its prewar state.

There are, of course, differences in the reequilibration processes following different wars, for since mobilization is the determinant of the magnitude of change, shorter wars and smaller mobilizations will effect smaller wartime changes and be followed by postwar reequilibrations to points closer to the prewar level. The greater the mobilization and the longer the war, the greater the transformations are likely to be. The massive mobilization for World War II entailed the greatest material changes in the structure of American society, affecting concentration and inequality more than any of the other three wars. The Vietnam War, because of its length and lack of threat, had the greatest impact on domestic cohesion.

Interestingly, the evidence provided by the United States experience in Vietnam suggests that partial demobilization during the course of conflict has much the same ramifications for domestic life as a full-scale postwar demobilization. During the war, the United States gradually reduced the number and role of its ground troops. As part of this process of "Vietnamization," the Nixon administration decreased the level of domestic mobilization while sustaining the war effort with Vietnamese bodies. Unlike a typical postwar demobilization, Vietnamization was neither immediate nor massive. Nonetheless, Vietnamization did effect a reversal in the wartime trends of the mobilization phase. Cohesion, which had decreased rapidly during the earlier war years, began to increase. The degree of inequality also began to climb after 1969, after having decreased during the first years of the war. Thus, the effects of Vietnamization resembled the more typical demobilization that follows a war's end, although, like the process itself, these effects were more gradual than those following the first three wars of the century.

Despite their limitations, these findings hold a number of lessons for policy-makers, making possible a more accurate assessment of war's unintended costs and benefits and at least allowing them to mobilize their nations for war more intelligently.

Wartime mobilization *always* affects domestic life, and the greater the mobilization effort, the larger the magnitude of change. War invariably leads to decreases in social cohesion and inequality at the same time that it increases the size of the state. When mobilization is very large, the scope of state power (political concentration) will also increase. During such a large-scale war effort, when increases in industrial and population concentration might also occur, the government can use its newly expanded powers to limit these changes.

More dramatically, policy-makers can avoid some of the effects of mobilization by eschewing it altogether. The modern nation, with a large government and standing peacetime army, can wage small wars without a special mobilization effort by diverting already extracted resources. In this way, it might well be possible to avoid effecting changes in concentration and inequality. Forgoing mobilization would not keep the war from decreasing cohesion, however, for war highlights the links between the costs and benefits of government, as the American experience in Vietnam makes quite clear. Once cognizant of the war effort, individuals connect the sacrifices they make with the benefits provided them in return. Even when the increased extraction is minimal or nonexistent, and individual sacrifice does not increase, people identify their standard peacetime burden with its new wartime application. Further, war efforts provide particularly obvious collective goods and costs, and this too decreases cohesion.

Eschewing mobilization can limit decreases in cohesion, since a war for which the government mobilizes the nation will suffer a greater loss of cohesion than an equally threatening war in which the challenge is met through the diversion of normally extracted resources. But decreases in cohesion cannot be fully avoided by minimal or zero mobilization unless the war is fought by mercenary soldiers in complete secrecy. As long as war is not waged in secret, however, individuals are acutely aware of the burdens they bear and the goods they receive in return. Thus, minimizing mobilization, or avoiding certain forms of mobilization, will not allow a society to avoid increased disunity. Lyndon Johnson's decision not to call up the reserves during the Vietnam War hardly spared the president or the nation the effects of decreased cohesion, and the elimination of the draft would not have eased national discord. Nor does the present lack of a draft suggest that the United States could wage war without engendering disunity; the loss of human life would remain visible. The families and friends of volunteers who die in war are not exempt from grief. Further, human labor is not the only resource extracted during wartime, and death is not the only cost. Taxes, inflation, and other forms of mobilization would still remain and would be visible, and the result would be the same, a wartime increase in disunity.

Partial (or minimal) wartime mobilization decreases not only cohesion but also the postwar size of the state. Individuals anticipate their contributions to the nation to shrink following the end of hostilities. When the resources used for waging war are primarily those diverted from their peacetime uses, only a decrease in the size of government will satisfy the expectations of the general public. For this reason, a negative displacement effect in the size of government is likely to follow any war in which the proportion of peacetime resources diverted to the war effort is greater than that of especially mobilized resources. Like the effects of mobilization on cohesion, this negative displacement effect can be avoided only by waging war in secret.

Mobilization is the critical mechanism through which war affects domestic life. Threat also affects national unity, however, even before the mobilization process gets underway. When the members of a society feel threatened, then the onset of war will immediately draw them together. Thus, when mobilization begins to decrease cohesion, it will be from the high point of unity achieved during the opening days of the war, and the extent of the decrease will be smaller than it would if there had been no threat.

When war is not perceived to involve threat (regardless of the actual existence of such danger), it will not serve to increase national solidarity at war's outset, and the extent of the decrease in cohesion will be greater. It may be possible that a skillful propaganda campaign can convince the public that there is a threat when none, in fact, exists. In this way, policy-makers may be able to mitigate, but not avoid, the costs of decreased cohesion.

As when threat exists, forgoing mobilization in a nonthreatening war provides only a partial solution to the wartime problems of decreased cohesion. Indeed, because decreases in cohesion are more extensive in nonthreatening wars, the minimization of mobilization is even less effective. In a nonthreatening and unpopular war, policy-makers can still lessen decreases in cohesion by a partial or full diversion of war-required resources from their normal peacetime uses. But their extraction would still rend the society more than would a massive mobilization in the face of threat, and would be likely to provoke protest as well.

The first requirement for policy-makers who want to avoid wartime decreases in cohesion is to enter only those wars that threaten the society. But to avoid decreased cohesion requires that the decreases in cohesion caused by wartime mobilization not exceed the initial increases in cohesion at the onset of a war in which the society is threatened. This can be accomplished by a mobilization that is so small that the decreases in cohesion it generates are exceeded by the increased cohesion generated at war's outset by the existence of threat. Alternatively, national leaders can undertake a massive mobilization to try to end the war quickly, since there is a lag before mobilization begins to decrease cohesion, and an even greater gap in time before the mobilization-induced decrease in cohesion exceeds the increase that the threat initially effected. This may well describe the wartime experiences of Israel, particularly the Six-Day War of 1967.

The perception of threat that allows for more extensive mobilization without catastrophic domestic consequences can thus be considered an aspect of a nation's war power, as can the mobilization itself. Steven Rosen argues that a state's war power is predicated on the society's willingness to suffer (cost-tolerance) as well as on its ability to harm (strength).[1] In a comparison of the strengths and cost-tolerances of warring nations (or coalitions) in seventy-seven wars during the last two centuries, Rosen finds that the superior cost-tolerance of the otherwise weaker nation can sometimes offset the greater military or material strength of the country with which it is at war. Strength is usually more important, but cost-tolerance can occasionally be decisive. For Rosen, the stronger state is the wealthier one, the one that extracts more revenue from its populace and is thus able to mobilize more extensively. He defines cost-tolerance, on the other hand, as the ability to withstand pain, and suggests that lower cost-tolerance may limit a nation's ability to mobilize. The discussion here, however, suggests that the process works both ways, that mobilization can serve to decrease cost-tolerance. Assuming that cohesion and cost-tolerance are directly related, it appears that the greater the material strength amassed by government for the war effort (i.e., mobilization), the greater will be the drop in cohesion and the less cost-tolerant the citizenry. If cost-tolerance and material strength are, in fact, inversely related, then the side that mobilizes more will always face a more cost-tolerant enemy.[2]

Of course the effect of mobilization on cohesion is itself variable, depending, for example, on the existence of threat. Thus, a differential cost-tolerance between two warring nations that is not explained by different mobilization patterns may well be explained by the fact that they have different perceptions of threat. It is this asymmetry in perceived threat that provides the materially weaker party with such superior cost-tolerance that it is able to win a war. Andrew Mack, author of a study of "why big nations lose small wars," discusses a number of such asymmetries, ones that explain the defeat of a presumably more powerful nation in war.[3] His list can, however, be reduced to the two discussed here. The first is asymmetry of mobilization, or as Rosen puts it, an asymmetry of material strength. A big nation in a small war, like the French in Algeria or the United States in Vietnam, has the potential to mobilize far more resources than its opponent. But often it does not, and the reason, according to Mack, involves the asymmetry of interests believed to be at stake.[4] This is, in fact, asymmetry of perceived threat. The smaller nation feels threatened; the big one does not. In addition to affecting cohesion directly, this differential perception also affects the consequences of mobilization. Mobilization by a threatened nation will decrease cohesion less than comparable mobilization by a nonthreatened one. An awareness of this fact, often a result of initial wartime experiences, can also affect mobilization. Thus, the big nation typically will not mobilize all the resources required for waging the war. The small nation can, however, mobilize more fully without suffering a comparable domestic fate. It is then the very asymmetry in perceived threat that results in the asymmetry of mobilization. And both of these explain "why big nations lose small wars."

The asymmetry of perceived threat may also play a role in war causation. Wars would not be fought if all parties were certain what the final outcome would be. But conflicting nations typically have different assessments of their relative power and are thus willing to risk going to war. The problem stems from the necessity of such assessments to include not only an appraisal of military and material strength but also an evaluation of the ability to mobilize and tolerate sacrifice—determinations that cannot be made a priori but only with regard for the actual circumstances of war initiation. Prior to World War II, for example, the Japanese found themselves in an intolerable position: American demands were unacceptable, but so was the American oil embargo. The Japanese thus contemplated initiating war before their situation deteriorated further. They knew that they would definitely lose if the United States mobilized fully, but reasoned that their only choice lay in a preemptive strike to cripple existing American military forces.[5] They hoped to force the United States to negotiate a settlement rather than wage a prolonged war requiring extensive domestic mobilization. Their miscalculation proved catastrophic. American leaders, who had been unable to involve the United States in either the Pacific or European wars as long as Americans felt unthreatened and secure, were now free to enter the war with full force. The preemptive Japanese attack on Pearl Harbor, on American soil, made possible the very extensive and extended mobilization that the Japanese feared. Without the sense of threat projected by the attack, the United States government may not have been able to undertake the mobilization of World War II, or would have been able to mobilize only with far greater domestic discord. The Japanese attack made possible the very things that the Japanese so feared, and doomed them to defeat. Their actions made it easy for American leaders to bring the full potential power of the United States to bear in the struggle.

The circumstances of war initiation are thus potentially central to the outcome. It is not enough to assess mobilization potential, for the same mobilization can have quite different effects on domestic cohesion depending on the existence of perceived threat. Moreover, initial domestic reaction can place limitations on the mobilization effort. Thus, the circumstances of war initiation and its effect on the perception of threat in the combatant nations can be critical in determining the outcome. It can explain not only why big nations lose small wars but also why aggressors in wars between two major powers may lose the very wars they begin.

This poses problems for a state's extension of its security sphere beyond its own borders. Major powers take many steps to demonstrate their commitments to protecting allies or pawns and deterring attacks on them.[6] The leaders of these protector nations often proclaim, for example, that they consider an attack on an ally to be equivalent to an attack on their own nation in order to signal the depth of their commitment. But the evidence here suggests that rushing to the defense of an attacked ally will have very different domestic ramifications than going to war in response to a direct attack. Leaders often bolster such alliance commitments, however, by placing their own troops on an ally's soil, insuring that the major power will also suffer casualties if the ally is attacked. The presence of such troops on foreign soil not only increases the credibility of the commitment and the strength of the alliance as deterrent, but may well increase the likelihood of domestic demands for revenge. It is not likely, however, that casualties suffered abroad will mitigate the costs of mobilization for a nation that is not itself attacked.

There are two modal contexts in which a nation goes to war. Its posture is either defensive (when it is attacked or when it strikes first as a preemptive tactic in a seriously threatening situation) or offensive (when it begins a war in times of security). In the first case, the nation typically undergoes full mobilization and yet avoids massive decreases in cohesion—even when the war is prolonged and extraction extensive. Cohesion will decrease, but the drop will be small given the size of mobilization, and the society will be relatively able to withstand it. Further, the growth of the state and the expansion of state powers allow the government to coordinate societal activity for the war effort. The postwar state will remain larger, and the society will stay more politically centralized.

When a nation begins an offensive war, on the other hand, there is little danger to the society, and war aims are at best related only indirectly to the basic security of the nation. In this context, policy-makers are confronted by more difficult problems concerning the mobilization process, which will clearly cause cohesion to decrease. As suggested above, any attempt to minimize the decrease by holding down the extent of the mobilization process will be only partly successful. Cohesion will decline, but less than it might in a full mobilization. As the American experience in Vietnam illuminates, such decreases can be massive even during a partial mobilization effort. In addition, undertaking a partial mobilization in order to mitigate the effects of waging war on national solidarity causes other problems for government leaders. Partial mobilizations, ones in which resources are diverted from their normal peacetime uses to the military effort, lead to a negative displacement effect in the size of government at war's end. Policy-makers must then choose either to protect the size of the state by mobilizing fully and accepting the greater decreases in cohesion that will accompany the war effort or to minimize decreases in cohesion and suffer a loss in state size as a result. The first policy may result in national dissent strong enough to topple the regime—the second may endanger the future role of the state in the society. Neither expense is small, and the choice is thus difficult; each alternative can have serious ramifications for both state and society.

Foreign adventurism is thus risky; it can carry grave costs and pose unattractive choices for political leaders. Those who contemplate initiating non-threatening wars would be wise to limit their nations' offensives to those in which victory will be quick and involve minimal sacrifices. If they cannot, the only other way to avoid the domestic ramifications of war is to wage it secretly and without mobilization.

The modern notion of limited war suggests another dimension along which wars can be delineated. The concept originated in the 1950s and refers to conflicts with constrained objectives and means. In limited wars, which can be either offensive or defensive, the military goals are the containment rather than defeat of the enemy, and the means are confined to exclude nuclear weapons. The Korean War began in the heyday of the Cold War with a massive sweeping assault against an American client state. The American people might have been convinced that there was some degree of threat, allowing the government to mobilize fully for the military effort. Such a limited war, accompanied by the perception of threat, can be fought without disastrous domestic consequences, and political critics focus on the existence of self-imposed limitations.

Yet to confine objectives and means in a limited war accompanied by threat may be akin to undercutting the belief that group effort can successfully deal with the danger. This belief is one of the conditions delineated in chapter 1 as necessary if external conflict is to increase internal cohesion. This condition, typically met for nations at war, may not exist in the limited wars of the nuclear age. If so, mobilization for limited war when threatened would engender greater decreases in cohesion per unit of mobilization than would mobilization for total war in the face of comparable threat.

The Vietnam War, on the other hand, is an example of a nonthreatening limited war. East West tensions were beginning to wane when the conflict began, and the American involvement did not appear to be a response to attack or to involve threat. Individual sacrifices were demanded for an effort that was not perceived to provide any benefit, in a context where no one believed that the limited group effort could successfully deal with the situation. The domestic results were disastrous.

For many policy analysts, one of the notable features of general war is that its domestic impact is symmetrical—it affects all members of a society equally. In addition, war involves the provision of goods that are not exclusively tangible, and war is therefore characterized by consensual elite politics. The analysis provided here can be put in the terms of this literature: if a war involves a threat that is symmetrical, then there will be a consensus that the society needs protection. The existence of the threat increases domestic cohesion throughout the society, including the political arena. But as this analysis also suggests, the very process of waging war involves the extraction of tangible goods and thus serves to decrease cohesion even if the impact of both threat and mobilization is symmetrical.

William Zimmerman, who suggests that general wars fall into the "arena of protection," argues that limited wars fall into a different class of political phenomena, one that he labels the "arena of redistribution."[7] Like general war, limited war involves the provision of goods that are not exclusively tangible. The domestic impact of a limited war is not symmetrical, however, and war policy is therefore characterized by conflictual elite politics. The fact that some are indulged and others are denied (asymmetrical impact), generates conflict among the decision-making elite. The analysis here, however, suggests that the severe domestic conflict generated by limited war develops precisely because mobilization is undertaken when there is no threat; such conflict is thus usually greater than that which occurs in general war and includes political manifestations. *This* is the asymmetry of limited war: the elite commit a society to war when the members of that society feel no threat. Moreover, the domestic conflict generated by mobilization for limited war is not confined to the elite but runs through the entire society.

The analysis here suggests, in other words, that symmetry involves the perception of threat but not necessarily mobilization. If the political elite finds a justification for war that is not shared by the citizenry, then wartime mobilization will generate political conflict. But even if threat is perceived by all, the very process of mobilization, because it involves the extraction of tangible goods, will decrease domestic cohesion even when the burden is equally distributed.

Waging war, one of the raisons d'être of the state, is a major governmental activity and preoccupies state planning in peace as well as state coordination during war itself. War is thus a major test for government as a political institution. The state's success in meeting this central challenge is a function of numerous factors, among them the kinds of wars in which it becomes involved. Offensive wars divorced from society's basic goals of security and self-preservation carry great domestic costs and pose serious problems for ruling elites. Yet, involvements in defensive wars, those in which the nation *is* threatened, are not without serious repercussions either. Threatened or not, the state and society both enjoy the unintended benefits and suffer the unintended costs of war. At the very least, policy-makers can insure that war's repercussions are not unanticipated.

NOTES

INTRODUCTION

1. Arthur A. Stein and Bruce Russett, "Evaluating War: Outcomes and Consequences," in *Handbook of Conflict Theory and Research,* ed. Ted Robert Gurr (New York: Free Press, 1980).

2. Arthur McDonald, "War and Criminal Anthropology," *Pan-American Magazine* 20 (February 1915): 24.

3. Calculated using international wars. See J. David Singer and Melvin Small, *The Wages of War, 1816–1965: A Statistical Handbook* (New York: John Wiley and Sons, 1972), pp. 152–55, table 7.1, column 9.

4. See the statistical appendix in Gil Elliot, *Twentieth-Century Book of the Dead* (New York: Scribner's, 1972).

5. James T. Shotwell, gen. ed., *Economic and Social History of the World War: Outline of Plan, European Series* (Washington: Carnegie Endowment for International Peace, 1924).

6. A list of the planned projects as of 1945 is in Shepard B. Clough, "Clio and Mars: The Study of World War II in America," *Political Science Quarterly* 60 (September 1945): 425–36.

7. Conclusion of an article reviewing the first decade of the single American behavioral social science journal devoted to "research related to war and peace." Elizabeth Converse, "The War of All Against All: A Review of the Journal of Conflict Resolution, 1957–1968," *Journal of Conflict Resolution* 12 (December 1968): 476–77.

8. David Walder, *The Short Victorious War: The Russo-Japanese Conflict, 1904–5* London: Hutchinson, 1973), p. 56.

9. Richard N. Rosecrance, *Action and Reaction in World Politics: International Systems in Perspective* (Boston: Little Brown and Company, 1963); and Arno Mayer, "Internal Causes and Purposes of War in Europe, 1870–1956," *Journal of Modern History* 41 (September 1969): 291–303.

10. Charles Tilly, "Reflections on the History of European State-Making," in *The Formation of National States in Western Europe,* ed. Charles Tilly (Princeton: Princeton University Press, 1975), p. 42.

CHAPTER 1

1. A. J. P. Taylor, *The Struggle for Mastery in Europe, 1848–1918* (London: Oxford University Press, 1954), chapters 8, 9.

2. See Alexander Kendrick, *The Wound Within: America in the Vietnam Years, 1945–1974* (Boston: Little, Brown and Company, 1974), on the American experience during the Vietnam War. Indeed, Richard Nixon, in his interview with David Frost, implied that his role was similar to Abraham Lincoln's in presiding over a severely divided nation.

3. The question arises as to whether such acts represent cohesion or the lack thereof. Some argue that governmental repression facilitates increased cohesion by supressing conflictual behavior. See Georg Simmel, "Conflict," trans. Kurt H. Wolff, in *Conflict and The Web of Group-Affiliations* (New York: The Free Press, 1955), which is one chapter of the 1923 edition of a 1908 work; Roberta Satow, "Political Repression During Wartime: An Empirical Study of Simmel's Theory of Conflict" (Ph.D. dissertation, New York University, 1972); and Keith F. Otterbein and Charlotte Swanson Otterbein, "An Eye for an Eye, a Tooth for a Tooth: A Cross-Cultural Study of Feuding," *American Anthropologist* 67 (December 1965): 1470–82. Terry Nardin has criticized this perspective, arguing that state violence should be studied as a form of political violence and not as a form of conflict management. See Terry Nardin, "Conflicting Conceptions of Political Violence," in *Political Science Annual: An International Review,* vol. 4, ed. Cornelius P. Cotter (Indianapolis: Bobbs-Merrill Company, 1973), pp. 75–126; and Terry Nardin, "Violence and the State: A Critique of Empirical Political Theory," *Sage Professional Papers in Comparative Politics* 2, 01–020 (1971).

An alternative perspective suggests that the individuals who comprise the governing elite evince conflictual behavior when they exercise repression, and that such behavior represents lessened cohesion. This is a difficult problem that involves at the most general level the question of whether force can create real attraction or just grudging compliance. It also raises the question of whether individuals in such situations would leave the group if able or remain despite an opportunity to leave.

On a more basic level, however, conflictual repressive actions represent decreased cohesion. It is certainly the case that if all individuals were attracted to the group, and that if none desired to break group norms, then such repression would not be necessary. Conflictual repression is thus a manifestation of decreased cohesion. Such repression may, however, be instrumental in indirectly decreasing conflictual behavior and thus increasing cohesion. To the extent that the punishment of criminals provides a deterrent to other would-be law-breakers, for example, then such an act of violence on the part of the state (i.e., the punishment) is instrumental in increasing cohesion. The point is that although the act itself is not cohesive, it can or does engender increased cohesion by discouraging certain forms of behavior. It should be noted, however, that certain other behavioral manifestations, those that cannot be so easily repressed or controlled, may increase instead. It is often easier to repress certain political institutions (e.g., third parties or antisystem parties) than it is to repress certain forms of political behavior (e.g., protests), and it is often easier to repress these political behaviors than it is to control other types of antisocial acts (e.g., crime), a consideration that is often taken into account by the governing elite.

Here, conflictual actions taken by the state will be treated like all other forms of conflictual behavior; although unlike other conflict it may be instrumental in increasing cohesion through deterrence. This relationship is modeled in the figure below, where C_1, C_2, C_3, C_4, and C_5 are indicators or manifestations of the lack of cohesions. The + sign linking the lack of cohesion to these indicators posits that any decrease in cohesion involves an increase in these various behaviors. The negative feedback link from C_5 to C_4 illustrates the independent dampening effect that governmental repression, itself an indicator of lack of cohesion, can have on other forms of behavior that are similarly indicative of the lack of cohesion.

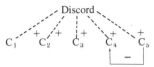

(Governmental Repression)

4. Raymond W. Mack and Richard C. Snyder, "The Analysis of Social Conflict—Toward an Overview and Synthesis," *Journal of Conflict Resolution* 1 (June 1957): 215.

5. The designation of general law was made by Ralf Dahrendorf, and cited in Robert A. LeVine and Donald T. Campbell, *Ethnocentrism: Theories of Conflict, Ethnic Attitudes, and Group Behavior* (New York: John Wiley and Sons, 1972), p. 31.

6. LeVine and Campbell, *Ethnocentrism*, p. 31.

7. See Louis Kriesberg, *The Sociology of Social Conflict* (Englewood Cliffs, N.J.: Prentice-Hall, 1973), p. 249; and Pitrim A. Sorokin, *Man and Society in Calamity: The Effects of War, Revolution, Famine, Pestilence Upon Human Mind, Behavior, Social Organization and Cultural Life* (New York: E. P. Dutton, 1942).

8. The following relies on Arthur A. Stein, "Conflict and Cohesion: A Review of the Literature," *Journal of Conflict Resolution* 20 (March 1976): 143–72.

9. In groups of any substantial size there are typically subgroups whose membership is wholly included in the larger collectivity. One problem that arises in this context is how subgroup cohesion affects the cohesion of the entire society. During wartime, this problem is particularly likely to arise in the context of repression; how are actions taken by the majority against another subgroup or by one smaller subgroup against another to be considered? An interesting wartime example is the incarceration of Japanese-Americans in internment camps during World War II.

The basic problem is to decide if a legal or physical legitimation of group divisions represents an increase or a decrease in cohesion. Those who claim that such actions serve to increase cohesion typically focus on the state of the majority. See Simmel, "Conflict," and Satow, "Political Repression During Wartime." Yet this position implicitly redefines group boundaries; the excluded subgroup is now considered to be alien, and its members are not seen as members (however deprived or second-class) of the original group at all. The problem here is that the comparison of cohesion at times t and t+1 actually involves the comparison of two different groups.

It is possible to compare a group at the two different points in time even if its membership is not entirely the same when its boundaries remained unchanged. The exclusion of a subgroup, however, changes the boundaries of the group in a way that natural population changes do not. Such an event involves more than a change in random personnel; it entails an actual redefinition of the group. Thus, if we are to compare the United States in 1943 to the United States in 1940, we must recognize the existence of Japanese-Americans as group members in both years. The fact that they had been repressed and removed from society does not mean that the society thus became more cohesive. Rather, it became less cohesive. The attempt to obtain cohesion by such boundary redefinition represents an increase in conflict and so serves to decrease cohesion when just the opposite is intended. If a minority subgroup is fully excluded by society (by death or deportation), it is possible to claim that the majority subgroup is more internally cohesive than was the entire society, and that the majority subgroup becomes more attracted to the society as a whole, which it now constitutes, than it was previously. It is not possible to compare the entire society at times t and t + 1, for it is, in fact, two different societies. Further, despite the increased cohesion of the majority subgroup, the exclusionary act itself remains disruptive and must be viewed independently of its consequence for a single subgroup. When the minority is only partly excluded, the internal cohesion of each subgroup is likely to increase. This change is not incorporated into the analysis of overall group cohesion, however, unless the subgroup's cohesion in some way affects that of the entire collectivity, in which case that group is studied directly.

10. Even when this is not technically the case, it is sometimes possible to consider a group to have existed, without nation status, prior to a war. The 1948 War of Independence clearly affected Israeli society, even though Israel did not yet exist as a nation at the outbreak of hostilities. The Jewish community in Palestine was, however, a self-conscious group with its own set of community institutions. Similarly, the American colonists' perceptions of British threat affected their society prior to the declaration of nationhood that followed the onset of armed conflict. And again, there is Bismarck's use of war to create a German nation. In the empirical test of this argument, however, only obviously extant nations are studied.

11. Only rarely is an internal source considered to be a danger to the nation. Sometimes those individuals who do not recognize an external threat blame another segment of the society for dragging the entire nation into the hostilities, a reaction that is itself evidence of discord. To this first subset, the only threat comes from the actual involvement in the war. There are other cases, however, usually toward the end of war, when a subgroup of the society sees a threat emanating from an internal as well as from an external source. This too may be evidence of decreased internal cohesion. McCarthyism, which began during a period of peace, grew dramatically during the Korean War. The danger was perceived to be a single one with a dual source; communism was believed to threaten from within the nation as well as from without. One reason for this phenomenon was frustration over the course of the war. Those who believed in the "omnipotent" America that they had seen emerge from World War II as the world's preeminent power were unable to cope with the concept of limited war. They recognized the existence of an external threat, but believed that the denial of total victory was evidence of internal treachery, in itself a threat. Such situations arise, however, only when defeat is avoided without the achievement of decisive victory.

12. Even if success if popularly predicted, it is unlikely that war will occur if there exists a knowledgeable elite who believes that victory is impossible to achieve. Thus, it has become a truism that one cause of war is the confidence of leaders on both sides. This is, in fact, so accepted an argument that scholars have repeatedly studied the Japanese decision to attack the United States in 1941 as an aberrant case in which the national leaders decided to go to war despite their correct prediction that they were going to lose. This was hardly the case with the general populace, however, and it is unlikely that they would have fought so willingly, if at all, had they been aware of and agreed with their leaders' assessment. The expectation of success is not always sustained, of course, and when war produces a decisive loser its people must at some point recognize their position. Even here there are exceptions; the Germans, for example, refused to accept their defeat in World War I. The empirical discussion, in Part II, is therefore limited to nations that either achieved clear success or avoided decisive defeat.

13. Nor is an imperial power likely to be threatened by a colonial war. It would be hard to argue, for example, that Britain was in any way threatened in the Boer War.

14. In the empirical work below, threat is treated as a dichotomous variable. It is assumed either to exist or not to exist for each of the nations involved in a given war.

15. In the empirical work that follows it is assumed that the existence of these requisites remains constant throughout the course of war; if they exist at the onset of conflict they do not change, and if they do not exist at the beginning of war then they do not appear later. Relaxing this assumption creates problems of estimation, but does not affect the logic of the theoretical and empirical work presented below. The reason a problem does not arise is that an additional proposition is presented below which argues that cohesion decreases as a function of the mobilization undertaken to wage war. Further, even when invariance is not assumed, it is argued that increases in the degree of perceived threat lead to increases in cohesion, but that decreases in threat will not cause cohesion to drop below its prewar level (if they lead to any decrease at all). Further, the onset of a nonthreatening war will neither increase nor decrease cohesion, although the mobilization process will effect domestic unity. Thus, relaxing the assumption of invariance in the level of perceived threat does not mean that variation in this determinant constitutes a rival explanation to the proposition that the process of mobilization serves to decrease domestic cohesion. It does, however, hamper the estimation of the marginal negative effect of mobilization on cohesion.

16. This discussion owes much to Anthony Downs, "Why the Government Budget is too Small in a Democracy," *World Politics* 12 (July 1960): 541–63.

17. Paul A. Samuelson, "The Pure Theory of Public Expenditure," *Review of Economics and Statistics* 36 (November 1954): 387.

18. Down, "Why the Government Budget is too Small," p. 547.

19. When individuals feel that the policy is an unwise one, they may not only resent the taxes but actually refuse to pay them. During the Vietnam War, some Americans resisted those taxes directly related to the war effort, such as the federal telephone tax. Others computed the proportion of their income taxes that went toward paying for the war and deducted these either through a "war crime deduction" or a "war crime credit." See Robert Calvert, comp. and ed., *Ain't Gonna Pay for War no More,* with a preface by Dave Dellinger (New York: War Tax Resistance, 1972).

20. Many of the studies of the causes of civil violence and rebellion focus on the absolute and relative deprivation of individuals. These studies can be related to this work if it is argued that wartime mobilization increases relative deprivation; i.e., if it increases the gap between what individuals receive and what they might have received had there been no process of extraction. The argument presented here may also be seen as operating on a different conceptual level, however. Here, the interest is in the frequency of manifestations of disaffection rather than the occurrence of one particular kind of disaffection.

21. This argument stresses the importance of the aggregate amount extracted in the mobilization process. This is not to suggest, however, that the way in which a mobilization effort is carried out is not also important. In particular, the means of a mobilization effort may affect a war's popularity, and government policy-makers must take this into account. During the Vietnam War, for example, the United States government refused to call up the reserves, despite the military establishment's desire to do so. The reason was that the use of reserves had proved to be highly unpopular during the Korean War, when many perceived it to be unfair. It is not argued here, however, that the way mobilization is effected directly affects cohesion, although it may affect manifestations of cohesion. Popularity and cohesion are not, of course, the same thing. See note 22 for discussion of this point.

22. It should be noted here that the support or popularity of a war effort is quite different from domestic cohesion. It may be that popularity, like cohesion, is affected by the perception of threat. In addition, some of the manifestations of cohesion may also be manifestations of a war's popularity. The concepts, however, are quite different. Again, it is argued here that cohesion will be negatively affected by the mobilization process—even in popular wars.

23. The argument here differs from that in the international relations linkage literature devoted to the study of the relationship between internal and external conflict behavior. The early linkage theorists referred to the theoretical sociological works on the effects of a group's involvement in an external conflict on changes in its internal cohesion. Unfortunately, however, their empirical work correlates a nation's internal conflict with its conflictual behavior toward others in the international system. Here, of course, the concern is with the effect of external threat directed at a nation with changes in its internal cohesion. Unless there is a perfect correlation between those hostilities directed at a nation and those directed by that nation toward others, then these works are irrelevent to the model here. Nor is it possible to use the model here as a theoretical justification for the linkage literature. For a more detailed discussion, see Arthur A. Stein, "Conflict and Cohesion," especially pp. 160–61.

24. Rudolph L. Truenfels, ed., *Eisenhower Speaks* (New York: Farrar, Straus and Company, 1948), p. 23.

CHAPTER 2

1. See Emory M. Thomas, *The Confederacy as a Revolutionary Experience* (Englewood Cliffs, N.J.: Prentice-Hall, 1971).

2. Etzioni has mistakenly included political centralization as part of his conceptualization of mobilization. Although he does not actually include political centraliza-

tion in his definition of mobilization, he does use it as an indicator of mobilization. Political centralization may be a good indicator if the causal process hypothesized in this chapter is confirmed, but the impression that Etzioni leaves is that political centralization is contained within mobilization rather than being caused by mobilization. For his views, see Amitai Etzioni, "Mobilization as a Macrosociological Conception," *British Journal of Sociology* 19 (September 1969): 252; see also Amitai Etzioni, "Societal Mobilization and Societal Change," in *The Active Society: A Theory of Societal and Political Processes* (New York: The Free Press, 1968), pp. 387–427.

3. James P. Baxter III, *Scientists Against Time* (Boston: Little, Brown and Company, 1946).

4. Robert Maynard Hutchins quoted by James L. Sundquist, *Politics and Policy: The Eisenhower, Kennedy, and Johnson Years* (Washington: The Brookings Institution, 1968), p. 180.

5. Increased concentration can also be a conscious element of public policy; see Arthur Robert Burns, "Concentration of Production," *Harvard Business Review* 21 (Spring 1943): 277–90. See also Charles A. Myers, "Wartime Concentration of Production," *Journal of Political Economy* 51 (June 1943): 222–34.

6. Frederic C. Lane, "Economic Consequences of Organized Violence," *Journal of Economic History* 18 (December 1958): 416.

CHAPTER 3

1. This is a common categorization scheme; see, for example, Celia S. Heller, ed., *Structured Social Inequality: A Reader in Comparative Social Stratification* (New York: Macmillan, 1969), part III; and R. K. Kelsall and Helen M. Kelsall, *Stratification: An Essay on Class and Inequality,* Aspects of Modern Sociology: Social Processes Series (London: Longman Group, 1974). Another classification is offered in Harold D. Lasswell and Arnold A. Rogow, *Power, Corruption and Rectitude* (Englewood Cliffs, N.J.: Prentice-Hall, 1963), p. 133; many of their categories can be subsumed by the typology presented here.

2. The focus here is narrower than that of Stanislav Andreski's *Military Organization and Society,* 2nd ed. (Berkeley and Los Angeles: University of California Press, 1968), in that this study focuses only on the impact of war and not on the impact of military organization in general. The conceptualization of participation employed here, however, is broader than Andreski's military participation ratio.

3. See Pitrim A. Sorokin, *Society, Culture, and Personality: Their Structure and Dynamics: A System of General Sociology* (New York: Harper and Brothers, 1947; reprint ed., New York: Cooper Square, 1969), p. 501; and Arthur L. Stinchcombe, "Some Empirical Consequences of the Davis-Moore Theory of Stratification," *American Sociological Review* 28 (October 1963): 805–8.

4. The effects of mobilization on participation (and thus on inequality) which are discussed above are visible and present in all wars. There are other such effects, however, that do not occur in all wars. Although all wars that involve conscription do affect the status of draftees by virtue of their participation in the military effort, for example, different types of wars affect those individuals in different ways. Typically, it is the young and the unskilled, those at or near the bottom of the various distri-

butional dimensions, who are drafted during the beginning of a conflict. And throughout the course of the war, it is those individuals who are sent to die. The highly skilled are often kept at home, sometimes deferred and sometimes drafted, to work on intelligence, do war-related research and development, or otherwise aid the war effort. Some of these skilled individuals do, of course, receive more dangerous assignments. Nonetheless, wartime armies are disproportionately composed of combat troops without civilian skills, and it is those below the median on the distributional dimensions who are impressed into military service. Again, the poor are disproportionately conscripted for military duty and thus suffer a disproportionate share of wartime casualties. See Robert E. Berney and Duane E. Leigh, "The Socioeconomic Distribution of American Casualties in the Indochina War: Implications for Tax Equity," *Public Finance Quarterly* 2 (April 1974): 223–35; and Duane E. Leigh and Robert E. Berney, "The Distribution of Hostile Casualties on Draft-Eligible Males with Differing Socioeconomic Characteristics," *Social Science Quarterly* 51 (March 1971): 932–40. Often draftees' incomes increase, and there have been studies to determine whether the draft has a progressive or regressive effect on income distribution. Some believe it to be progressive, whereas others argue that it affects only some income ranges in a progressive fashion; see Robert E. Berney, "The Incidence of the Draft—Is it Progressive?" *Western Economic Journal* 7 (September 1969): 244–47. A more appropriate analysis to determine this redistributive effect of mobilization would include those who enlist precisely in order to obtain a better deal than they would if they waited to be drafted.

In popular wars (typically those in which a threat to society is perceived by most group members), those in military service, including these lower-status draftees, rise in social standing. It should be noted, of course, that war popularity and wartime social cohesion are not the same thing. The argument in chapter 1 is that cohesion decreases during the course of all wars as a function of mobilization, irrespective of the war's popularity. It is conceivable that individuals who resent their increased contributions toward the provision of a collective good nonetheless support the war. They clearly do recognize the war effort as providing a good and defer to those who pay disproportionately for its provision.

In these cases, therefore, the greater the level of mobilization, the lesser the degree of inequality, since there are more participants who rise along the distributional dimensions by virtue of their participation in the military aspects of the war effort. In unpopular wars, however, this effect is not observed at all; the Vietnam War is an example of a nation's involvement in an external conflict not only failing to bring honor and increased social standing to its military personnel but actually causing them to be disrespected by many of their fellow citizens.

5. The conclusion is that of Neil A. Wynn, "The impact of the Second World War on the American Negro," *Journal of Contemporary History* 6, no. 2 (1971): 51. The two authors quoted by Wynn (ibid., p. 42) are John Hope Franklin and Gunnar Myrdal, respectively.

6. It is possible to consider individuals to be socially produced and distributed goods in that their chances of survival and quality of life are differentially affected by public policies on abortion, health, medical care, and conscription. This argument is not made here, however.

7. The above discussion owes much to Richard Titmuss, "War and Social Policy," in *Essays on "The Welfare State"* (London: Allen and Unwin, 1958), pp. 77–82.

CHAPTER 4

1. These wars (and the others investigated) have been chosen because they are interesting examples that allow for controlled analysis given the constraint of data availability. Data constraints will come into sharper focus as the analysis progresses. Observations should, of course, be chosen to maximize variance in the independent variables, and this chapter, therefore, describes the variance in the independent variables for these cases.

2. Cases must also be chosen so as to control for plausible rival hypotheses. One way to do this is to match observations for values on the plausible rivals. In other words, if X_2 is a plausible rival to X_1 as a determinant of changes in Y, then one way to validate the effect of X_1 is to look at the covariation of X_1 and Y while controlling for the value of X_2. Thus, observations should be chosen in order to maximize variance in X_1 but hold constant the values of X_2—to control for the effects of X_2 by holding it invariant.

3. There are two good reviews of this literature: Richard W. Leopold, "The Problem of American Intervention, 1917: An Historical Retrospect," *World Politics* 2 (April 1950): 405–25; and Daniel M. Smith, "National Interest and American Intervention, 1917: An Historiographical Appraisal," *Journal of American History* 52 (June 1965): 5–24.

4. The two quotations are the conclusions of Richard W. Van Alstyne and Edward M. Earle, respectively, and are quoted in Leopold, "The Problem of American Intervention," pp. 422–23.

5. Smith, "National Interest and American Intervention," p. 24.

6. A recent critique is Bruce M. Russett, *No Clear and Present Danger: A Skeptical View of the United States Entry into World War II* (New York: Harper and Row, 1972). For reviews of the literature on American entry into World War II, see Wayne S. Cole, "American Entry into World War II: A Historiographical Approach," *Mississippi Valley Historical Review* 43 (March 1957): 595–617; and Justus D. Doenecke, "Beyond Polemics: An Historiographical Re-Appraisal of American Entry into World War II," *The History Teacher* 12 (February 1979): 217–51.

7. John E. Mueller, *War, Presidents and Public Opinion* (New York: John Wiley and Sons, 1973), pp. 168–69.

8. United States, Bureau of the Budget, Committee on Records of War Administration, War Records Section, *The United States at War: Development and Administration of the War Program by the Federal Government* (Washington: Bureau of the Budget, 1946; reprint ed., New York: Da Capo Press, 1972), p. 47.

9. Ibid., p. 89.

10. Mueller, *War, Presidents and Public Opinion*, pp. 45, 48.

11. The longer the war and the greater the wartime inflation, the greater will be the percentage of the prewar national income constituted by the cost of the war. In constant dollar figures, the total incremental costs of the Vietnam War came to 17.8 percent of the national income in 1964, as opposed to the 20.8 percent that was obtained from

current dollar figures in table 4-1. The figures are computed from data provided by Robert Warren Stevens, *Vain Hopes, Grim Realities: The Economic Consequences of the Vietnam War* (New York: New Viewpoints, 1976), p. 92.

12. U.S., Department of Defense, OASD (Comptroller), Directorate for Information Operations and Control, *Selected Manpower Statistics* (Washington: Department of Defense, June 1976), p. 60. This covers the period January 1, 1965 through March 31, 1973.

13. During the Korean War, there was a drop in the number of total military personnel on active duty from 1952 to 1953. The reason for this is that the data in figure 4-1 are as of June 30 of each year, and by June 1953 the war was very close to ending.

Total military personnel on active duty, rather than military expenditures, is used here as an indicator for mobilization. This is because the former is available as a continuous data series whereas the government has calculated the latter in different ways at different times. Moreover, the correlation between total military personnel and the best possible series on military expenditures (in constant dollars) which can be constructed for the period 1900–72 is .95.

14. Given the large peacetime army sustained by the United States following the end of World War II, it might seem that total military personnel does not accurately reflect fluctuations in the Vietnam War mobilization. The correlation of total military personnel on active duty and military personnel in South Vietnam (on June 30 of each year) for the period 1965–72 is .95. The correlation of total military personnel on active duty and military personnel in South Vietnam (on December 31) for the same period is .99. The correlation of total military personnel on active duty and yearly incremental war costs for the period 1965–72 is .77. It is clearly appropriate to use total military personnel as an indicator of mobilization.

CHAPTER 5

1. To test whether the occurrence of an event has an effect on the temporal variation of a dependent variable, it is necessary only to have indicators of cohesion which are compiled comparably for each temporal unit. It is acceptable to use different indicators of a single concept for different nations, or to use the same indicators for different nations even if they are defined differently or gathered differently in those nations. Similarly, different indicators (or differently defined indicators) may be used in the separate analyses of one nation's data in different time periods. In this project, therefore, the only requirement is that the data used for each nation/war be comparable across time within designated periods.

The research design utilized in this endeavor is one form of quasi-experimental design. For discussions of this research design see a number of the items in section 6 of the bibliography.

Most ex post facto covariation research designs used in the social sciences require that all the determinants of the dependent variable be known and incorporated into the explanatory model, or at least that the unincorporated determinants be uncorrelated with the included ones. Otherwise, conclusions about the effects of any independent variables are biased. The great inferential strength of experimental designs, on the other hand, is that it is possible to make inferences about the existence of an effect of any independent variable without knowledge of any other determinants by controlling observational variance and by employing randomized assignment. Quasi-experimental research designs utilize the logic of experimental designs with regard to ex post facto data. This project utilizes a weak form of quasi-experimental design, the single inter- rupted time-series design. The purpose is to ascertain whether the occurrence of war has effected changes in the time-series of a dependent variable.

The methodology of interrupted time-series is to fit atheoretical curves to the time series of the dependent variable and then use a dummy variable to estimate whether the observations assumed to be affected by the occurrence of some event are significantly different from the expectation derived from the movement of the series prior to the occurrence of the event.

In this project, one regression equation has been estimated for an entire series with trend and dummy variables used for the nonwar and war periods rather than estimating separate regression lines for war and nonwar periods and then testing for step-level and slope changes between periods. In this way, it is possible to estimate directly step and slope change coefficients as well as standard errors. Indeed, it is possible to manipulate the independent variable series so that various changes can be estimated. If, for example, there are successive war and nonwar periods, fitting separate trend lines allows the estimation of the actual slope of the second nonwar period trend line, or its slope difference from the immediately preceding war period, or its slope difference from the previous nonwar period. Similar flexibility exists in estimating step-level changes.

In almost all cases, fitting a series of trend lines to war and nonwar periods has resulted in an R^2 upwards of 95 percent. Thus, more complex curve fitting procedures have not been necessary. Moreover, presentation of the interrupted time-series regres- sion results is necessary only for the empirical work in this chapter, where the effects of two determinants are estimated. In the empirical chapters that follow, reporting the results of interrupted time-series regressions is not necessary. The data meet the interocular test of significance; the effects, or lack thereof, of the occurrence of war on a series are readily visible.

2. For a discussion of the logic of multiple measurement of a concept, see Donald T. Campbell, "Definitional Versus Multiple Operationism," *et al.* 2 (Summer 1969): 14–17.

3. The violent crime rate is composed of four crimes: murder and nonnegligent manslaughter, forcible rape, robbery, and aggravated assault. It is used in this analysis because the data are comparable over time. These various activities were criminal during the entire period under discussion. Thus, any change in the incidence of these crimes in wartime is not artifactual. Some argue that crime increases in wartime because certain behaviors, such as black market activities, draft dodging, or antiwar activities, are either newly defined as criminal or are prosecuted when they have previously been ignored. These behaviors are still, of course, manifestations of de- creased cohesion. Nonetheless, it is necessary to use the same yardstick for the nonwar and war periods. There is a basic agreement, however, that wartime violations of specific war acts are generally common; see Edwin H. Sutherland, "Crime," in *American Society in Wartime,* ed. William Fielding Ogburn (Chicago: University of

Chicago Press, 1943), pp. 191–92. See also Marshall B. Clinard, "Criminological Theories of Violations of Wartime Regulations," *American Sociological Review* 11 (June 1946): 258–70.

4. See Marvin E. Wolfgang and Franco Ferracuti, *The Subculture of Violence: Towards an Integrated Theory in Criminology* (London: Tavistock Publications, 1967), pp. 258, 317–18.

5. Dane Archer and Rosemary Gartner, "Violent Acts and Violent Times: A Comparative Approach to Postwar Homicide Rates," *American Sociological Review* 41 (December 1976): 943, refer to this plausible rival hypothesis as the baby-boom artifacts model. They reject this alternative explanation for increases in American crime in the late 1960s by examining data on the age of persons arrested for homicide and determining that all age groups show an increase in such arrests during the Vietnam War.

6. This is not the amount of crime committed by young people. Rather, the total number of violent crimes committed in the society is divided by the number of resident individuals in the fifteen-to-twenty-four-year-old bracket (as opposed to the normal crime rate calculation, in which the total number of violent crimes is divided by the total population). The use of resident youth population also controls for changes in the crime rate wrought by the sending abroad of young people as part of the military effort.

7. The model developed in chapter 1 predicts fluctuations in the occurrence of manifestations of discord. For this reason, a frequency measure, rather than the duration and size measures that are also available, is used for work stoppages.

Recently, there have been a number of works focusing on the "shape" of strikes, a three-dimensional solid that represents the strike profile of a society. The three dimensions, frequency, duration, and size, are multiplied in order to create a single composite measure of strike volume. The problem with this measure is that the concept of volume has no status; it is appealing strictly because it is all inclusive. There are strong theoretical and empirical grounds for differentiating the determinants of the occurrence of strikes from the determinants of their duration, severity, or size. Examples of the use of the shape and volume conceptions of strike activities are Edward Shorter and Charles Tilly, "The Shape of Strikes in France, 1830–1960," *Comparative Studies in Society and History* 13 (January 1971): 60–86; and Douglas A. Hibbs, Jr., "Industrial Conflict in Advanced Industrial Society," *American Political Science Review* 70 (December 1976): 1033–58. An empirical work that shows that there are indeed different determinants for these factors is Jack W. Skeels, "Measures of U.S. Strike Activity," *Industrial and Labor Relations Review* 24 (July 1971): 515–25. In addition, David Britt and Omer H. Galle, "Industrial Conflict and Unionization," *American Sociological Review* 37 (February 1972): 46–57, analyze the relative contributions of each component to the composite variable and also find that exogenous variables have differential impacts on the various components. The strike data have not been controlled for the size of the system. One reason is that it is not clear which of several possible controls (such as the size of the labor force, the number of business establishments, the number of unionized workers, the degree of unionization, or average union size) is most appropriate. In addition, there is a long tradition of studying the actual number of strikes.

8. Michael Stohl, "War and Domestic Political Violence: The Case of the United States 1890–1970," *Journal of Conflict Resolution* 19 (September 1975): 387. His

definition excludes criminal acts and excludes nonviolent strikes (which his discussion suggests are the majority of work stoppages).

9. Since the number of domestic conflict events is only available through 1970, the average for the period 1935–70 was inserted as the value for 1971 and 1972. This is a conservative procedure for estimating missing values since its impact is to allow the 1971 and 1972 factor score values to be determined solely by the other measures, crime and strikes.

10. The estimated coefficients for World War II and the Korean War are in the predicted direction (i.e., negative) but are insignificant. The significant negative coefficient obtained for the Vietnam War is artifactual. The actual observations (figure 5-1) show no such step-level decrease at the war's outset. Because of the increases in the crime rate in 1963 and 1964, the fitted trend line for the pre–Vietnam War period leads to an overly large predicted value for the 1966 observation (the first war observation). At the same time, given the massive increase in the series during the war, the fitted curve provides a very low fitted value for the same observation. The combination of these two factors gives rise to an artifactual estimated coefficient.

11. For the Vietnam War, the coefficient is greater than zero with more than 99.9 percent certainty. The coefficient for World War II is greater than zero with more than 99.5 percent certainty. For the Korean War, the degree of certainty that the coefficient is greater than zero is slightly less than 75 percent.

12. The coefficients are estimates of the marginal propensity for discord as a function of mobilization. The number of military personnel on active duty is used here as the measure of mobilization. As noted in chapter 4, the number of military personnel overestimates the number of individuals who actually served in the war zone. This is true in every war, but is magnified in the Korean and Vietnam cases. When the actual number of military personnel serving in the war zone is used as the measure of mobilization, then the Korean coefficient is even larger relative to the World War II coefficient than the one reported here. The Vietnam coefficient is still larger. Nevertheless, the number of military personnel is the most desirable measure of mobilization, since it does measure the number of individuals who are drawn into the military in wartime. Even though many may never serve in the war area, the possibility always exists, and both those in service and those remaining at home recognized this fact.

13. The table below presents the correlation of yearly battle deaths and cumulative battle deaths with three measures of military personnel for the American involvement in the Vietnam War for the years 1965–72.

Correlations of Measures of U.S. Battle Deaths and Measures of U.S. Military Personnel, 1965–72

	Battle Deaths	Cumulative Battle Deaths
Total military personnel on active duty (as of June 30)	.93	−.12
Military personnel in Vietnam (as of June 30)	.88	.19
Military personnel in Vietnam (as of December 31)	.92	−.22

Sources: See sources in figure 4-1. In the second source listed there, pp. 59–60 were also used.

14. John E. Mueller, *War, Presidents and Public Opinion* (New York: John Wiley and Sons, 1973), pp. 63, 65. For a critique of Mueller's work which reaffirms the negative impact of war on presidential popularity, see Samuel Kernell, "Explaining Presidential Popularity: How Ad Hoc Theorizing, Misplaced Emphasis, and Insufficient Care in Measuring One's Variables Refuted Common Sense and Led Conventional Wisdom Down the Path of Anomalies," *American Political Science Review* 72 (June 1978): 506–22.

15. This drop occurred in both the House of Representatives and the Senate, and is revealed not only by the percentage of votes in which a majority of Democrats opposed a majority of Republicans, but also by the percentage of votes that were not unanimous. See table 5-4.

16. Studies of war Congresses clearly detail the growth of partisanship (within limits) during the wars; see Seward W. Livermore, *Politics is Adjourned: Woodrow Wilson and the War Congress, 1916–1918* (Middletown, Conn.: Wesleyan University Press, 1966); and Roland Young, *Congressional Politics in the Second World War* (New York: Columbia University Press, 1956; reprint ed., New York: Da Capo Press, 1972).

17. Edwin E. Witte, "Strikes in Wartime: Experience With Controls," *The Annals of the American Academy of Political and Social Science* 224 (November 1942): 128–34.

18. Shorter and Tilly, "Shape of Strikes in France."

19. Albert Rees, "Industrial Conflict and Business Fluctuations," *Journal of Political Economy* 60 (October 1952): 382.

20. Ernest H. Jurkat and Dorothy B. Jurkat, "Economic Function of Strikes," *Industrial and Labor Relations Review* 2 (July 1949): 531.

21. The quote is from Betty B. Rosenbaum, "The Relation Between War and Crime in the United States," *Journal of the American Institute of Criminal Law and Criminology* 30 (January–February 1940): 738. See the items on war and crime in section 2b of the bibliography.

22. As this trend shows, increases in the crime rate during the 1960s were not a function of the coming of age of the children born in the baby boom following World War II. Nor is it the case, as is often assumed, that the 1960s crime wave was largely a racial phenomenon. Rather, there were similar increases in the commission of violent crimes by older as well as younger citizens, by both whites and blacks, and by women as well as men; see U.S., Executive Office of the President: Office of Management and Budget, *Social Indicators 1973* (Washington: Government Printing Office, 1973), pp. 69–70, tables 2/13, 2/14.

23. Such increases in crime have occurred in defeated and occupied nations as well as in victorious, unoccupied ones. Varying war experiences, however, have been credited as the determinants of changes in wartime crime rates; see Hermann Mannheim, *War and Crime* (London: Watts and Company, 1941), pp. 74–75; Pitrim Sorokin, *Contemporary Sociological Theories* (New York: Harper and Brothers, 1928), pp. 341–42; Walter A. Lunden, *Crimes and Criminals* (Ames: Iowa State University Press, 1967), p. 77; and Sutherland, "Crime," p. 197. Since it is not possible to derive here an expected relationship for these determinative factors, they have been controlled for in the choice of observations.

24. Archer and Gartner, "Violent Acts and Violent Times," p. 942; Thorsten Sellin, *Research Memorandum on Crime in the Depression* (New York: Social Science Research Council, Committee on Studies in Social Aspects of the Depression, Bulletin 27, 1937), pp. 61–62; and Sutherland, "Crime," pp. 199–200.

25. Hermann Mannheim, *Comparative Criminology: A Text Book* (London: Routledge and Kegan Paul, 1965), p. 595.

26. Walter Bromberg, "The Effects of the War on Crime," *American Sociological Review* 8 (December 1943): 685, and Mannheim, *Comparative Criminology,* p. 595, respectively.

27. Archer and Gartner, "Violent Acts and Violent Times." An earlier study of just World War I reached the same conclusion; see Thorsten Sellin, "Is Murder Increasing in Europe?" *The Annals of the American Academy of Political and Social Science* 125 (May 1926): 29–34.

28. This assumes, of course, that battle deaths constitute a rough measure of mobilization and that the existence of threat is equal across both subsets (those with both higher and lower casualties).

Battle deaths are not strictly a measure of the amount of mobilization undertaken by government for waging war, for although governments extract individuals, they do not extract life. Deaths are a direct function of war, but not of the mobilization process undertaken to wage it. Nevertheless, cumulative mobilization is one determinant of cumulative battle deaths since the greater the mobilization, the more individuals impressed, and the greater the number that may die. Just as obviously, there are other determinants of the number of battle deaths, but cumulative mobilization is one of them, and thus they are correlated. Using cumulative battle deaths to rank-order the mobilizations of the four American wars in the twentieth century would provide a similar rank-ordering to that obtained in chapter 4. The table below compares the two indicators of cumulative mobilization discussed in chapter 4 with total battle deaths.

U.S. Mobilization and Battle Deaths in Four Twentieth-Century Wars

War	Original Incremental Cost as % of National Income in Prewar Year	% of Prewar Population Serving during the War	Total Battle Deaths
World War II	355.1	11.2	291,557
World War I	70.5	4.6	53,402
Vietnam War	20.8	4.5	45,941
Korean War	24.8	3.8	33,629

Sources: See tables 4-1 and 4-2. U.S. Department of Defense, OASD (Comptroller), Directorate for Information Operations and Control, *Selected Manpower Statistics* (Washington: Department of Defense, June 1976), p. 61.

29. In addition to controlling for plausible rival hypotheses, it is important to discuss seemingly contradictory evidence. William H. Flanigan and Edwin Fogelman, "Patterns of Political Violence in Comparative Historical Perspective," *Comparative Politics* 3 (October 1970): 1–20, perform an extensive longitudinal analysis of patterns of political violence. They find that "there is no general pattern of either positive or negative interrelationship between war and domestic political violence" (p. 5). Briefly, they determined decennial scores for foreign military involvements of indi-

vidual nations as well as for their levels of domestic political violence. Given the differentiation here between different kinds of wars and given the way in which cohesion can increase and then decrease, it would appear that lumping all domestic political violence, and indeed all wars, into one score for each country for each decade might effectively obscure any existing relationship.

30. Warren Schaich, "A Relationship Between Collective Racial Violence and War," *Journal of Black Studies* 5 (June 1975): 377.

31. Marvin D. Krohn, "Inequality, Unemployment and Crime: A Cross-National Analysis," *Sociological Quarterly* 17 (Summer 1976): 303–13, and Paul E. Spector, "Population Density and Unemployment: The Effects of the Incidence of Violent Crime in the American City," *Criminology* 12 (February 1975): 399–401.

32. It might be argued that inequality is a more plausible rival determinant here than is concentration. Domestic inequality is often assumed to lead to individual disaffection with the society. The traditional argument is that increased inequality leads to increased disaffection, and decreased inequality leads to decreased disaffection. It is argued here that wartime mobilization leads to increased disaffection and decreased inequality. If inequality does indeed decrease in wartime, then it would be expected to mitigate disaffection, not to exacerbate it. Thus, inequality is not a rival to mobilization as a determinant of increased disaffection, although its omission from the model leads to an underestimation of the marginal propensity for disaffection.

Some argue that disaffection increases when a group has experienced success and their expectations begin to outstrip their achievements. Thus, even decreases in inequality might increase the disaffection of those whose standing has improved. The problem is that this does not really explain wartime decreases in cohesion at all. According to this view, manifestations of discord should increase when the expected decreases in inequality generated by mobilization are no longer sustained and individual expectations outstrip the possibilities for achievement. This increase would not be expected to occur until late in a war, when the economic hardships of mobilization are most apparent and when mobilization no longer generates decreased inequality. At that point, however, the increase should be spectacular. Although it is shown in this chapter that wartime decreases in cohesion are often sustained into the immediate postwar period, it is also clear that there is a marked decrease in the manifestations of disaffection when wars end. This pattern is the reverse of that predicted by such a model.

33. The correlation between the percent increase in violent crime and net migration is .29. Even if it is argued that regions that experience a net loss of population should also suffer from turmoil and thus experience an increase in violent crime, the correlation between the percent increase in the violent crime rate and the absolute value of net migration is .29.

34. Spector, "Population Density and Unemployment"; and Robert B. Hagedorn, Jon P. Miller, and Sanford Labovitz, "Industrialization, Urbanization and Deviant Behavior: Examination of Some Basic Issues," *Pacific Sociological Review* 14 (April 1971): 177–95.

35. Schaich, "Relationship Between Collective Racial Violence and War," p. 376.

CHAPTER 6

1. For a discussion of the various measures of societal production, see U.S., Bureau of the Census, *Historical Statistics of the United States, Colonial Times to 1970* (Washington: Government Printing Office, 1976), pp. 215–17.

2. The size of government will fail to increase in wartime only when there is no mobilization at all, i.e., when the government diverts resources already at its command for war purposes.

3. The correlation between total direct federal expenditures as a percentage of GNP (table 6-3) and the percentage of the civilian labor force employed by the federal government (figure 6-2) for the years available between 1913 and 1974 is .88. For the years 1929–74, the correlation between federal purchases of goods and services as a percentage of GNP (figure 6-1) and the percentage of the civilian labor force employed by the federal government (figure 6-2) is .81. For the available years between 1932 and 1974, the correlation between federal expenditures as a percentage of GNP (table 6-3) and federal purchases of goods and services as a percentage of GNP (figure 6-1) is .79.

4. In addition to federal expenditures as a percentage of GNP, data on federal purchases of goods and services as a percentage of GNP are presented in figure 6-1. This is in order to meet the objection of those who argue that total federal expenditures do not measure the public claim on output. Total federal expenditures include transfer payments and interest on the public debt, both of which are considered nonexhaustive expenditures since they are not a claim on output. Federal purchases of goods and services, or exhaustive expenditures, are an accurate measure of the public claim on output. Using federal expenditures as a percentage of GNP in order to measure the fluctuation of the federal sector may therefore lead to erroneous conclusions. The federal sector is necessarily larger after a war since nonexhaustive expenditures such as veterans' benefits and interest on the war debt are larger following a conflict than before it. For this reason, data on federal purchases of goods and services are provided in order to show that the larger federal sectors of most postwar periods are real, ones that do involve a larger claim on output. For the distinction between exhaustive and nonexhaustive expenditures, see Francis M. Bator, *The Question of Government Spending: Public Needs and Private Wants* (New York: Harper and Brothers, 1960).

5. The "displacement effect" is developed by Alan T. Peacock and Jack Wiseman, *The Growth of Public Expenditure in the United Kingdom* (Princeton, N.J.: Princeton University Press, 1961). For a critique, see Frederic L. Pryor, *Public Expenditures in Communist and Capitalist Nations* (Homewood, Ill.: Richard D. Irwin, Inc., 1968), pp. 443–46.

6. This point can be expanded. Those who posit a displacement effect follow in the tradition of those who argue that the origins of the state are rooted in the requisites of survival (the ability to wage war being a central element), and that the optimum size of the state is determined by the requisites of waging war. See Robert L. Carneiro, "A Theory of the Origin of the State," *Science,* August 21, 1970, pp. 733–38; Richard

Bean, "War and the Birth of the Nation State," *Journal of Economic History* 33 (March 1973): 203–21; and Robert E. Park, "The Social Function of War," *American Journal of Sociology* 46 (January 1941): 551–70. See also Joseph A. Schumpeter, "The Crisis of the Tax State," trans. W. F. Stolper and R. A. Musgrave, in *International Economic Papers, No. 4: Translations Prepared for the International Economic Association,* ed. Alan T. Peacock, Wolfgang F. Stolper, Ralph Turvey, and Elizabeth Henderson (New York: Macmillan, 1954), pp. 5–38.

7. The measurement procedure here is slightly different from but comparable to Pryor's "centralization ratio." See Pryor, *Public Expenditures,* pp. 26–27, 70ff.

8. Such estimates are provided in U.S., Congress, Senate, Temporary National Economic Committee, *Investigation of Concentration of Economic Power,* monograph no. 4: *Concentration and Composition of Individual Incomes, 1918–1937,* by Adolph J. Goldenthal, Senate Committee Print, 76th Cong., 3d sess., 1940, p. 83.

9. An analysis of net farm migration reveals a similar pattern. In other words, the results presented in the table are unaffected by differential birth and death rates.

10. U.S., Bureau of the Census, "Internal Migration in the United States: April, 1940, to April 1947," *Current Population Reports,* series P-20, no. 14 (April 15, 1948), p. 13.

11. For a brief discussion of black migration during World War I, see John Hope Franklin, *From Slavery to Freedom: A History of Negro Americans,* 3rd ed. (New York: Alfred A. Knopf, 1967), pp. 471–73. See also the items he cites in his bibliographic essay, p. 675.

12. Such a comparison of the yearly proportions of assets held by the largest firms controls for secular inflation, since it is assumed that inflation affects the value of all corporate assets in the same magnitude as it affects the assets of the largest firms. For a discussion of limitations of this measure, see A. D. H. Kaplan, *Big Enterprise in a Competitive System* (Washington: The Brookings Institution, 1954), pp. 115–17. Some scholars use just information on the assets of manufacturing firms, but this too has its deficiencies.

13. Kaplan, *Big Enterprise,* p. 31.

14. Quoted in ibid., p. 32.

15. Ibid. For an example of wartime thinking about such issues, see A.D.H. Kaplan, *The Liquidation of War Production: Cancellation of War Contracts and Disposal of Government-owned Plants and Surpluses,* Committee for Economic Development Research Study (New York: McGraw-Hill Book Company, 1944).

16. Kaplan, *Big Enterprise,* pp. 33ff.

CHAPTER 7

1. B. R. Mitchell, *European Historical Statistics 1750–1970* (New York: Columbia University Press, 1975), pp. 168, 171, table C2.

2. Clarence D. Long, *The Labor Force in Wartime America,* Occasional Paper 14 (New York: National Bureau of Economic Research, March 1944), p. 39.

3. Clarence D. Long, *The Labor Force in War and Transition: Four Countries,* Occasional Paper 36 (New York: National Bureau of Economic Research, 1952).

4. Long, *Labor Force in Wartime America.*

5. In addition, it may be that the return to participants is relative to the degree of their participation, and that the degree of participation of certain sets of individuals increases in wartime; see Mark Abrahamson, "Functionalism and the Functional Theory of Stratification: An Empirical Assessment," *American Journal of Sociology* 78 (March 1973): 1236–46.

6. Robinson G. Hollister and John L. Palmer, "The Impact of Inflation on the Poor," in *Redistribution to the Rich and the Poor: The Grants Economics of Income Distribution,* ed. Kenneth E. Boulding and Martin Pfaff (Belmont, Calif.: Wadsworth Publishing, 1972), p. 253; Ann R. Horowitz, "The Pattern and Causes of Changes in White-Nonwhite Income Differences: 1947–1972," in *Patterns of Racial Discrimination,* vol. 2: *Employment and Income,* ed. George M. von Furstenberg, Ann R. Horowitz, and Bennett Harrison (Lexington, Mass.: D. C. Heath and Company, 1974), pp. 150, 158; Ann R. Horowitz, "Trends in the Distribution of Family Income within and between Racial Groups," in *Employment and Income,* p. 203; Charles E. Metcalf, "The Size Distribution of Personal Income During the Business Cycle," *American Economic Review* 59 (September 1969): 657 68; T. Paul Schultz, "Secular Trends and Cyclical Behavior of Income Distribution in the United States: 1944–1965," in *Six Papers on the Size Distribution of Wealth and Income,* ed. Lee Soltow (New York: National Bureau of Economic Research, 1969), p. 87; and Lester C. Thurow, "Analyzing the American Income Distribution," *American Economic Review* 60 (May 1970): 261–69.

7. Harold Lydall, *The Structure of Earnings* (Oxford: Clarendon Press, 1968), pp. 169–71; Frederic Meyers, "Notes on Changes in the Distribution of Manufacturing Wage Earners by Straight-Time Hourly Earnings, 1941–1948," *Review of Economics and Statistics* 32 (November 1950): 352–55; Schultz, "Secular Trends," p. 86; Lester C. Thurow, *Generating Inequality: Mechanisms of Distribution in the U.S. Economy* (New York: Basic Books, 1975); Wayne Vroman, "Changes in Black Workers' Relative Earnings: Evidence from the 1960s," in *Employment and Income,* pp. 167–96.

8. Elizabeth K. Nottingham, "Toward an Analysis of the Effects of Two World Wars on the Role and Status of Middle-Class Women in the English-Speaking World," *American Sociological Review* 12 (December 1947): 666–75. Also see Mary Anderson, "Women's Status in Industry in World War 2," in *Yearbook of American Labor,* vol. 1: *War Labor Policies,* ed. Colston E. Warne, Warren B. Catlin, Dorothy W. Douglas, J. Raymond Walsh, and Constance Williams (New York: Philosophical Library, 1945), pp. 414–21.

9. These are not, of course, the only means of extraction. In addition to extracting income, governments may requisition other types of goods directly. Further, they may choose to raise extra revenue by borrowing, most typically by floating war bonds. Only rarely, however, can a war be entirely financed by loans. Further, borrowing typically degenerates into inflation; see Franz B. Wolf, "Economy in War Time," in *War in the Twentieth Century,* ed. Willard Waller (New York: Dryden Press, 1940), pp. 381ff.

10. Hollister and Palmer, "Impact of Inflation," p. 253; Metcalf, "Size Distribution of Personal Income"; William D. Nordhaus, "The Effects of Inflation on the

Distribution of Economic Welfare," *Journal of Money, Credit, and Banking* 5 (February 1973): 465–504; and Thurow, "Analyzing the American Income Distribution," p. 263.

11. Alfred H. Conrad, "Redistribution Through Government Budgets in the United States, 1950," in *Income Redistribution and Social Policy: A Set of Studies,* ed. Alan T. Peacock (London: Jonathan Cape, 1954), pp. 200, 237–38; Selma F. Goldsmith, "Impact of the Income Tax on Socio-Economic Groups of Families in the United States," in *Income Redistribution and the Statistical Foundations of Economic Policy,* ed. Colin Clark and Geer Stuvel (New Haven, Conn.: International Association for Research in Income and Wealth, 1964), p. 271; Richard A. Musgrave, Karl E. Case, and Herman Leonard, "The Distribution of Fiscal Burdens and Benefits," *Public Finance Quarterly* 2 (July 1974): 259–311; Joseph A. Pechman "Distribution of Income Before and After Federal Income Taxes, 1941 and 1947," in *Studies in Income and Wealth,* vol. 13: *Conference on Research in Income and Wealth* (New York: National Bureau of Economic Research, 1951), p. 194; Benjamin A. Okner, "Individual Taxes and the Distribution of Income," in *The Personal Distribution of Income and Wealth,* ed. James D. Smith (New York: National Bureau of Economic Research, 1975), pp. 45–73; and Charles Stauffacher, "The Effect of Government Expenditures and Tax Withdrawals upon Income Distribution, 1930–1939," in *Public Policy,* ed. C. J. Friedrich and Edward S. Mason (Cambridge, Mass.: Harvard University, Graduate School of Public Administration, 1941), pp. 232–61.

12. Selma F. Goldsmith, "Statistical Information on the Distribution of Income by Size in the United States," *American Economic Review* 40 (May 1950): 326–27; Metcalf, "Size Distribution of Personal Income"; and Dorothy S. Projector, Gertrude S. Weiss, and Erling T. Thoresen, "Composition of Income as Shown by the Survey of Financial Characteristics of Consumers," in *Six Papers,* ed. Soltow, p. 111.

13. Daniel Creamer, *Personal Income During Business Cycles* (Princeton, N.J.: Princeton University Press, 1956), p. 110, argues that there were indeed major gains in labor income during and immediately following World War I.

14. See Horowitz, "Pattern and Causes of Changes," p. 158. Howard P. Tuckman and Gary Brosch, "Changes in Personal Income and Their Effect on Income Shares," *Southern Economic Journal* 41 (July 1974): 78–86, on the other hand, argue that this measure is problematic.

15. Conrad, "Redistribution Through Government Budgets"; Phillips Cutright, "Income Redistribution: A Cross-National Analysis," *Social Forces* 46 (December 1967): 180–90; Norval D. Glenn, "Social Security and Income Redistribution," *Social Forces* 46 (June 1968): 538–39; Musgrave, Case, and Leonard, "Distribution of Fiscal Burdens"; Okner, "Individual Taxes"; Benjamin A. Okner, "Transfer Payments: Their Distribution and Role in Reducing Poverty," in *Redistribution to Rich and Poor,* ed. Boulding and Pfaff, pp. 62–77; Thurow, "Analyzing the American Income Distribution," p. 263; and Harold L. Wilensky, *The Welfare State and Equality: Structural and Ideological Roots of Public Expenditures* (Berkeley and Los Angeles: University of California Press, 1975), p. 87.

There is a similar consensus on the redistributional effect of all governmental expenditures, not just those for social services; see John H. Adler, "The Fiscal System, the Distribution of Income, and Public Welfare," in *Fiscal Policies and the American*

Economy, ed. Kenyon E. Poole (New York: Prentice-Hall, 1951), pp. 359–409; W. Irwin Gillespie, "Effect of Public Expenditures on the Distribution of Income," in *Essays in Fiscal Federalism,* ed. Richard A. Musgrave (Washington: The Brookings Institution, 1965), pp. 122–86; Thurow, "Analyzing the American Income Distribution," p. 263; and Rufus S. Tucker, "The Distribution of Government Burdens and Benefits," *American Economic Review* 43 (May 1953): 518–34.

16. This is not inconsistent with the results of empirical studies of the opportunity costs of defense expenditures. See Frederic L. Pryor, *Public Expenditures in Communist and Capitalist Nations* (Homewood, Ill.: Richard D. Irwin, Inc., 1968); Bruce M. Russett, "Who Pays for Defense?" *American Political Science Review* 63 (June 1969): 412–26; Bruce M. Russett, *What Price Vigilance? The Burdens of National Defense* (New Haven, Conn.: Yale University Press, 1970), pp. 127–56; Jerry Hollenhorst and Gary Ault, "An Alternative Answer to: Who Pays for Defense?" *American Political Science Review* 65 (September 1971): 760–63; David A. Caputo, "New Perspectives on the Public Policy Implications of Defense and Welfare Expenditures in Four Modern Democracies: 1950–1970," *Policy Sciences* 6 (December 1975): 423–46; and David Dabelko and James M. McCormick, "Opportunity Costs of Defense: Some Cross-National Evidence," *Journal of Peace Research* 14 (1977): 145–54. The argument here is simply that there is no decrease in aggregate federal social welfare expenditures in wartime.

17. Two surveys of historical studies of U.S. income distribution are Dorothy S. Brady, "Measurement and Interpretation of the Income Distribution in the United States," in *Income and Wealth: Series VI,* ed. Milton Gilbert and Richard Stone (London: Bowes and Bowes, 1957), pp. 78–97, and C. L. Merwin, Jr., "American Studies of the Distribution of Wealth and Income," in *Studies in Income and Wealth,* vol. 3, Conference on Research in National Income and Wealth (New York: National Bureau of Economic Research, 1939), pp. 30–84.

18. Rufus S. Tucker, "The Distribution of Income Among Income Taxpayers in the United States, 1863–1935," *Quarterly Journal of Economics* 52 (August 1938): 558–59.

19. Ibid., p. 586.

20. For a discussion of the inverse Pareto slope, see Lee C. Soltow, "Evidence on Income Inequality in the United States, 1866–1965," *Journal of Economic History* 29 (June 1969): 279–80.

21. What is referred to here as the Gini inequality measure is more typically known as the Gini concentration ratio. For a brief discussion of this measure, see James Morgan, "The Anatomy of Income Distribution," *Review of Economics and Statistics* 44 (August 1962): 281. There are dozens of books and articles evaluating and comparing measures of inequality. For one recent work with an extensive bibliography, see F. A. Cowell, *Measuring Inequality: Techniques for the Social Sciences* (New York: John Wiley and Sons, 1977). In addition, see Hayward R. Alker, Jr., and Bruce M. Russett, "Indices for Comparing Inequality," in *Comparing Nations: The Use of Quantitative Data in Cross-National Research,* ed. Richard L. Merritt and Stein Rokkan (New Haven, Conn.: Yale University Press, 1966), pp. 349–72; James Caporaso, "Methodological Issues in the Measurement of Inequality, Dependence, and Exploitation," in *Testing Theories of Economic Imperialism,* ed. Steven J. Rosen and James

R. Kurth (Lexington, Mass.: D. C. Heath and Company, 1974), pp. 87–114; Joseph L. Gastwirth, "Statistical Measures of Earnings Differentials," *The American Statistician* 29 (February 1975): 32–35; Corrado Gini, "Measurement of Inequality of Incomes," *Economic Journal* 31 (March 1921): 124–26; Carl Morris, *Measures of Relative Income Inequality* (Santa Monica, Calif.: Rand Corporation, R-1026-RC, May 1972); and W. S. Woytinsky, "Methods of Measuring Inequality in Individual Earnings," in *Earnings and Social Security in the United States* (Washington: Social Science Research Council, Committee on Social Security, 1943), pp. 1–16.

22. Horst Menderhausen, *Changes in Income Distribution During the Great Depression* (New York: National Bureau of Economic Research, 1946).

23. See, for example, Tucker, "Distribution of Income."

24. For discussions on the availability and comparability of the various data sources for the U.S. size distribution of income see Goldsmith, "Statistical Information"; Selma F. Goldsmith, "Appraisal of Basic Data Available for Constructing Income Size Distributions," in *Studies in Income and Wealth,* 13: 266–373; Helen Swanson, "A Guide to Income Distributions," *The Conference Board Record* 17 (July 1960): 48–51; U.S., Congress, Joint Economic Committee, Subcommittee on Economic Statistics, *The Distribution of Personal Income: A Study of Statistics on the Size Distribution of Personal Income in the United States,* by T. Paul Schultz (December 1964), pp. 49–104. One attempt to reconcile two different definitions of income is by John C. Hinrichs, "The Relationship Between Personal Income and Taxable Income," *Survey of Current Business* 55 (February 1975): 3335.

25. When Lorenz curves (the basis for computing the Gini measure) for different years do not intersect, there exists no possibility that the Gini measures for those years would not reflect, or would distort, changes in inequality. As there is no overlap here, there is no need to provide measures of inequality other than the Gini. The Lorenz curves for 1935/36, 1941, 1944, and 1950 are graphed in Selma Goldsmith, George Jaszi, Hyman Kaitz, and Maurice Liebenberg, "Size Distribution of Income Since the Mid-Thirties," *Review of Economics and Statistics* 36 (February 1954): 8.

26. For discussions of American inequality for the period 1929–50, see Goldsmith, "Statistical Information"; Goldsmith et al., "Size Distribution of Income"; Bernard F. Haley, "Changes in the Distribution of Income in the United States," in *The Distribution of National Income,* ed. Jean Marchal and Bernard Ducros (New York: St. Martin's Press, 1968), pp. 3–21; Robert J. Lampman, "Recent Changes in Income Inequality Reconsidered," *American Economic Review* 44 (June 1954): 251–68; and Pechman, "Distribution of Income."

27. Goldsmith et al., "Size Distribution of Income," p. 17, graphically displays the lessened inequality in the distribution of wage-salary families in 1944 as compared with 1935/36. See also Haley, "Changes in the Distribution of Income," p. 20.

28. The importance of the participation rate is especially stressed by the 1949 *Economic Report of the President*; see Herman P. Miller, "Factors Related to Recent Changes in Income Distribution in the United States," *Review of Economics and Statistics* 33 (August 1951): 214. The impact of taxation is stressed by Mary W. Smelker, "Shifts in the Concentration of Income," *Review of Economics and Statistics* 30 (August 1948): 219. On the increasingly progressive nature of the tax system during this period see Tucker, "Distribution of Government Burdens."

29. Smelker, "Shifts in the Concentration of Income," p. 219.

30. Edward C. Budd, "Postwar Changes in the Size Distribution of Income in the U.S.," *American Economic Review* 60 (May 1970): 247; Haley, "Changes in the Distribution of Income," p. 5; U.S., Bureau of the Census, *Income Distribution in the United States,* by Herman P. Miller (Washington: Government Printing Office, 1966), p. 22; Schultz, "Secular Trends," p. 98; Martin Schnitzer, *Income Distribution: A Comparative Study of the United States, Sweden, West Germany, East Germany, the United Kingdom, and Japan* (New York: Praeger Publishers, 1974), p. 39.

31. For observations on American inequality during the Korean War period, see Selma F. Goldsmith, "Changes in the Size Distribution of Income," *American Economic Review* 47 (May 1957): 514–15; and Metcalf, "Size Distribution of Personal Income," p. 660.

32. For a discussion of the redundancy measure of inequality, see Horowitz, "Trends in the Distribution of Family Income," pp. 199–201.

CONCLUSION

1. Steven Rosen, "War Power and the Willingness to Suffer," in *Peace, War, and Numbers,* ed. Bruce M. Russett (Beverly Hills, Calif.: Sage Publications, 1972), pp. 167–83; see also Steven Rosen, "A Model of War and Alliance," in *Alliance in International Politics,* ed. Julian R. Friedman, Christopher Bladen, and Steven Rosen (Boston: Allyn and Bacon, 1970), pp. 215–37.

2. Assuming that the parameter linking cohesion and mobilization is the same across all nations.

3. Andrew Mack, "Why Big Nations Lose Small Wars: The Politics of Asymmetric Conflict," *World Politics* 27 (January 1975): 175–200.

4. A. F. K. Organski and Jacek Kugler, "Davids and Goliaths: Predicting the Outcomes of International Wars," *Comparative Political Studies* 11 (July 1978): 141–80, argue that seemingly more powerful nations lose wars precisely because their opponents bring more capabilities to the struggle either through foreign aid or by greater domestic extractive effort. Their empirical work, however, compares not absolute levels of national capability but a measure of residual extraction from an averaged expectation. Thus, they do not accurately test their own verbal theory.

5. For transcripts of Japanese prewar discussions, see Nobutaka Ike, ed., *Japan's Decision for War: Records of the 1941 Policy Conferences* (Stanford, Calif.: Stanford University Press, 1967).

6. Bruce M. Russett, "The Calculus of Deterrence," *Journal of Conflict Resolution* 7 (June 1963): 97–109; Thomas C. Schelling, *Arms and Influence* (New Haven, Conn.: Yale University Press, 1966), chapter 2.

7. William Zimmerman, "Issue Area and Foreign Policy Process: A Research Note in Search of a General Theory," *American Political Science Review* 67 (December 1973): 1204–12.

SELECTED
BIBLIOGRAPHY

1. EFFECTS OF WAR: GENERAL

Andreski, Stanislav. *Military Organization and Society*. 2nd ed. Berkeley and Los Angeles: University of California Press, 1968.

Clough, Shepard B. "Clio and Mars: The Study of World War II in America." *Political Science Quarterly* 60 (September 1945): 425–36.

Dewey, Edward R., and Dakin, Edwin F. "War and Its Dislocations." In *Cycles: The Science of Prediction*, pp. 200–14. New York: Henry Holt and Company, 1947.

Doti, James. "The Response of Economic Literature to Wars." *Economic Inquiry* 16 (October 1978): 616–26.

Dunn, David. "War and Social Change." In *The Use of Force in International Relations*, pp. 220–47. Ed. F. S. Northedge. New York: The Free Press, 1974.

Klein, Lawrence R. "The Role of War in the Maintenance of American Economic Prosperity." *Proceedings of the American Philosophical Society* 115 (December 1971): 507–16.

Lane, Frederic C. "The Economic Meaning of War and Protection." *Journal of Social Philosophy and Jurisprudence* 7 (April 1942): 254–70.

Leeds, Anthony. "The Functions of War." In *Science and Psychoanalysis*, vol. 6: *Violence and War*, pp. 69–82. Ed. Jules H. Masserman. New York: Grune and Stratton, 1963.

Marwick, Arthur. "The Impact of the First World War on British Society." *Journal of Contemporary History* 3 (January 1968): 51–63.

_____. *War and Social Change in the Twentieth Century: A Comparative Study of Britain, France, Germany, Russia and the United States*. New York: St. Martin's Press, 1974.

Nef, John U. *War and Human Progress: An Essay on the Rise of Industrial Civilization*. Cambridge, Mass.: Harvard University Press, 1950.

125

Nelson, Keith L. *The Impact of War on American Life: The Twentieth-Century Experience*. New York: Holt, Rinehart and Winston, 1971.

Ogburn, William. "Are Our Wars Good Times?" In *On Culture and Society*, pp. 269-85. Chicago: University of Chicago Press, 1964.

Park, Robert E. "The Social Function of War." *American Journal of Sociology* 46 (January 1941): 551-70.

Shotwell, James T., gen. ed. *Economic and Social History of the World War: Outline of Plan, European Series*. Washington: Carnegie Endowment for International Peace, 1924.

Sorokin, Pitrim. "Social Functions and the Effects of War and Struggle." In *Contemporary Sociological Theories*, pp. 328-52. New York: Harper and Brothers, 1928.

———. *Social and Cultural Dynamics*. Vol. 3: *Fluctuation of Social Relationships, War, and Revolution*. New York: The Bedminster Press, 1937.

———. *Man and Society in Calamity: The Effects of War, Revolution, Famine, Pestilence upon Human Mind, Behavior, Social Organization and Cultural Life*. New York: E. P. Dutton and Company, 1942.

———. "The Social and Cultural Effects of War Upon the Belligerent Nations and Other Groups." In *Society, Culture, and Personality: Their Structure and Dynamics*, pp. 499-502. New York: Cooper Square Publishers, 1969.

Winter, J. M., ed. *War and Economic Development: Essays in Memory of David Joslin*. New York: Cambridge University Press, 1975.

Wright, Chester W. "The More Enduring Economic Consequences of America's Wars." *Journal of Economic History*, supplement (December 1943): 9-25.

2. WAR AND COHESION

A. CONFLICT, MOBILIZATION, AND COHESION

Barton, Allen H. *Social Organization Under Stress: A Sociological Review of Disaster Studies*. Washington: National Academy of Sciences, National Research Council, 1963.

Berman, Paul. *Revolutionary Organization: Institution-Building Within the People's Armed Forces*. Lexington, Mass.: D. C. Heath and Company, 1974.

Bernard, Jessie. "Some Current Conceptualizations in the Field of Conflict." *American Journal of Sociology* 70 (January 1965): 442-54.

Bottomore, T. B. "Sociological Theory and the Study of Social Conflict." In *Theoretical Sociology: Perspectives and Developments*, pp. 137-53. Ed. John C. McKinney and Edward A. Tiryakian. New York: Appleton-Century-Crofts, 1970.

Cartwright, Dorwin. "The Nature of Group Cohesiveness." In *Group Dynamics: Research and Theory*, pp. 91-109. 3rd ed. Ed. Dorwin Cartwright and Alvin Zander. New York: Harper and Row, 1968.

Collins, Randall. *Conflict Sociology: Toward an Explanatory Science*. New York: Academic Press, 1975.

Coser, Lewis. *The Functions of Social Conflict*. New York: The Free Press, 1956.

Dahrendorf, Ralf. "Toward a Theory of Social Conflict." *Journal of Conflict Resolution* 2 (June 1958): 170-83.

Etzioni, Amitai. "Mobilization as a Macrosociological Conception." *British Journal of Sociology* 19 (September 1968): 243–53.

———. "Societal Mobilization and Societal Change." In *The Active Society: A Theory of Societal and Political Processes,* pp. 387–427. New York: The Free Press, 1968.

Fink, Clinton F. "Some Conceptual Difficulties in the Theory of Social Conflict." *Journal of Conflict Resolution* 12 (December 1968): 412–60.

Fritz, Charles E. "Disaster." In *Contemporary Social Problems: An Introduction to the Sociology of Deviant Behavior and Social Disorganization,* pp. 651–94. Ed. Robert K. Merton and Robert A. Nisbet. New York: Harcourt, Brace and World, 1961.

Hamblin, Robert L. "Group Integration During a Crisis." *Human Relations* 11 (February 1958): 67–76.

International Sociological Association. *The Nature of Conflict: Studies on the Sociological Aspects of International Tensions.* Paris: UNESCO, 1957.

Janis, Irving L. "Group Identification Under Conditions of External Danger." *British Journal of Medical Psychology* 36 (1963): 227–38.

Kriesberg, Louis *The Sociology of Social Conflict.* Englewood Cliffs, N.J.: Prentice-Hall, 1973.

Lanzetta, John T. "Group Behavior Under Stress." *Human Relations* 8 (February 1955): 29–52.

———, Haefner, Don, Langham, Peter, and Axelrod, Howard. "Some Effects of Situational Threat on Group Behavior." *Journal of Abnormal and Social Psychology* 49 (July 1954): 445–53.

LeVine, Robert A., and Campbell, Donald T. *Ethnocentrism: Theories of Conflict, Ethnic Attitudes, and Group Behavior.* New York: John Wiley and Sons, 1972.

Lott, Albert J., and Lott, Bernice E. "Group Cohesiveness as Interpersonal Attraction: A Review of Relationships with Antecedent and Consequent Variables." *Psychological Bulletin* 64 (October 1965): 259–309.

Mack, Raymond W., and Snyder, Richard C. "The Analysis of Social Conflict— Toward an Overview and Synthesis." *Journal of Conflict Resolution* 1 (June 1957): 212–48.

Mintz, Alexander. "Non-Adaptive Group Behavior." *Journal of Abnormal and Social Psychology* 46 (April 1951): 150–59.

Murphy, Robert F. "Intergroup Hostility and Social Cohesion." *American Anthropologist* 59 (December 1957): 1018–35.

Otterbein, Keith F. "Cross-Cultural Studies in Armed Combat." *Buffalo Studies* 4 (April 1968): 91–109.

———. "The Anthropology of War." In *Handbook of Social and Cultural Anthropology,* pp. 923–58. Ed. John J. Honigmann. Chicago: Rand McNally, 1973.

Pepitone, Albert, and Kleiner, Robert. "The Effect of Threat and Frustration on Group Cohesiveness." *Journal of Abnormal and Social Psychology* 54 (March 1957): 192–99.

Powell, Elwin H. *The Design of Discord: Studies of Anomie.* New York: Oxford University Press, 1970.

Sherif, Muzafer. *In Common Predicament: Social Psychology of Intergroup Conflict and Cooperation.* Boston: Houghton Mifflin Company, 1966.

Simmel, Georg. "Conflict." Trans. Kurt H. Wolff. In *Conflict and The Web of Group-Affiliations*, pp. 11–123. Foreword by Everett C. Hughes. New York: The Free Press, 1955.

Stein, Arthur A. "Conflict and Cohesion: A Review of the Literature." *Journal of Conflict Resolution* 20 (March 1976): 143–72.

Sumner, William Graham. *Folkways*. Boston: Ginn, 1906.

Turner, Jonathan H. "From Utopia to Where: A Critique of the Dahrendorf Conflict Model." *Social Forces* 52 (December 1973): 236–44.

———. "A Strategy for Reformulating the Dialectical and Functional Theories of Conflict." *Social Forces* 53 (March 1975): 433–44.

———. "Marx and Simmel Revisited: Reassessing the Foundations of Conflict Theory." *Social Forces* 53 (June 1975): 618–27.

Williams, Robin M., Jr. *The Reduction of Intergroup Tensions*. Bulletin No. 57. New York: Social Science Research Council, 1947.

B. WAR AND CRIME

Abbott, Edith. "Crime and the War." *Journal of the American Institute of Criminal Law and Criminology* 9 (May 1918): 32–45.

———. "The Civil War and the Crime Wave of 1865–1870." *Social Service Review* 1 (June 1927): 212–34.

———. "Juvenile Delinquency During the First World War: Notes on the British Experience, 1914–1918." *Social Service Review* 17 (June 1943): 192–212.

Archer, Dane, and Gartner, Rosemary. "Violent Acts and Violent Times: A Comparative Approach to Postwar Homicide Rates." *American Sociological Review* 41 (December 1976): 937–63.

Blackmar, F. W. "Does War Increase Crime?" *Proceedings of the National Conference of Social Work* (1918): 121–24.

Bromberg, Walter. "The Effects of the War on Crime." *American Sociological Review* 8 (December 1943): 685–91.

Clinard, Marshall B. "Criminological Theories of Violations of Wartime Regulations." *American Sociological Review* 11 (June 1946): 258–70.

Darrow, Clarence. "War and Crime." In *Crime: Its Causes and Treatment*, pp. 213–20. New York: Thomas Y. Crowell Co., 1922.

Exner, Franz. *Krieg und Kriminalitat in Osterreich* [War and Criminality in Austria]. New Haven, Conn.: Yale University Press, 1927.

Glueck, Eleanor T. "Wartime Delinquency." *Journal of Criminal Law and Criminology* 33 (July-August 1942): 119–35.

Hacker, M. E. "The Influence of the World War on Crime." *Revue Internationale de Droit Penal* 4 (1927): 95–109.

International Penal and Penitentiary Commission. *The Effects of the War on Criminality*. Berne: Staempfli & Cie., 1951.

Liepmann, Moritz. *Krieg und Kriminalitat in Deutschland* [War and Criminality in Germany]. New Haven, Conn.: Yale University Press, 1930.

Lunden, Walter A. "Wars and Criminality." In *Crimes and Criminals*, pp. 71–97. Ames: Iowa State University Press, 1967.

Mannheim, Hermann. "Crime in Wartime England." *Annals of the American Academy of Political and Social Science* 217 (September 1941): 128-37.

_____. *War and Crime*. London: Watts and Company, 1941.

_____. "Some Reflections on Crime in War-time." *Fortnightly* 151 (January 1942): 38-46.

_____. "The Effects of Wars." In *Comparative Criminology: A Text Book*, pp. 591-99. London: Routledge and Kegan Paul, 1965.

Matthews, M. Alice. "The Effect of War on the Criminal Tendencies of the Race." Washington: Carnegie Endowment for International Peace Library, August 1934.

Merrill, Francis E. "War and Crime." In *Social Problems on the Home Front: A Study of War-time Influences*, pp. 169-99. New York: Harper and Brothers, 1948.

Neumeyer, Martin H. "Delinquency Trends in Wartime." *Sociology and Social Research* 29 (March-April 1945): 262-75.

Parsons, Charles. "The Influence of the War on Crime." In *Proceedings of the Annual Congress of the American Prison Association: 1917*, pp. 266-68. Indianapolis: William B. Burford, 1917.

Porterfield, Austin L. "A Decade of Serious Crime in the United States: Some Trends and Hypotheses." *American Sociological Review* 13 (February 1948): 44-54.

Reckless, Walter C. "The Impact of War on Crime, Delinquency and Prostitution." *American Journal of Sociology* 48 (November 1942): 378-86.

Rosenbaum, Betty B. "The Relation Between War and Crime in the United States." *Journal of the American Institute of Criminal Law and Criminology* 30 (January-February 1940): 722-40.

Sellin, Thorsten. "Is Murder Increasing in Europe?" *The Annals of the American Academy of Political and Social Science* 125 (May 1926): 29-34.

_____. "War and Crime: A Research Memorandum." Committee on Research on Social Aspects of the War. New York: Social Science Research Council, September 1942.

Sutherland, Edwin H. "Crime." In *American Society in Wartime*, pp. 185-206. Ed. William Fielding Ogburn. Chicago: University of Chicago Press, 1943.

Wiers, Paul. "Wartime Increases in Michigan Delinquency." *American Sociological Review* 10 (August 1945): 515-23.

Willbach, Harry. "Crime in New York City as Affected by War." *Journal of Criminal Law and Criminology* 34 (March-April 1944): 371-76.

C. STRIKES

Britt, David, and Galle, Omer H. "Industrial Conflict and Unionization." *American Sociological Review* 37 (February 1972): 46-57.

Eldridge, J. E. T. "Explanations of Strikes." In *Industrial Disputes: Essays in the Sociology of Industrial Relations*, pp. 12-67. London: Routledge and Kegan Paul, 1968.

Hansen, Alvin H. "Cycles of Strikes." *American Economic Review* 11 (December 1921): 616-21.

Hibbs, Douglas A., Jr. "Industrial Conflict in Advanced Industrial Society." *American Political Science Review* 70 (December 1976): 1033-58.

———. "On the Political Economy of Long-Run Trends in Strike Activity." *British Journal of Political Science* 8 (April 1978): 153–75.

Jurkat, Ernest H., and Jurkat, Dorothy B. "Economic Function of Strikes." *Industrial and Labor Relations Review* 2 (July 1949): 527–45.

Rees, Albert. "Industrial Conflict and Business Fluctuations." *Journal of Political Economy* 60 (October 1952): 371–82.

Ross, Arthur M., and Irwin, Donald. "Strike Experience in Five Countries, 1927–1947: An Interpretation." *Industrial and Labor Relations Review* 4 (April 1951): 323–42.

Shorter, Edward, and Tilly, Charles. "The Shape of Strikes in France, 1830–1960." *Comparative Studies in Society and History* 13 (January 1971): 60–86.

———. *Strikes in France, 1830–1968.* Cambridge: Cambridge University Press, 1974.

Skeels, Jack W. "Measures of U.S. Strike Activity." *Industrial and Labor Relations Review* 24 (July 1971): 515–25.

Snyder, David. "Early North American Strikes: A Reinterpretation." *Industrial and Labor Relations Review* 30 (April 1977): 325–41.

———, and Tilly, Charles. "Hardship and Collective Violence in France, 1830 to 1960." *American Sociological Review* 37 (October 1972): 520–32.

Stearns, Peter N. "Measuring the Evolution of Strike Movements." *International Review of Social History* 19, part 1 (1974), pp. 1–27.

Taylor, George W. "Labor's No Strike Pledge—A Statistical View." In *Yearbook of American Labor,* vol. 1: *War Labor Policies,* pp. 137–42. Ed. Colston E. Warne, Warren B. Catlin, Dorothy W. Douglas, J. Raymond Walsh, and Constance Williams. New York: Philosophical Library, 1945.

Weintraub, Andrew R. "Prosperity versus Strikes: An Empirical Approach." *Industrial and Labor Relations Review* 19 (January 1966): 231–38.

Witte, Edwin E. "Strikes in Wartime: Experience with Controls." *The Annals of the American Academy of Political and Social Science* 224 (November 1942): 128–34.

Yoder, Dale. "Economic Changes and Industrial Unrest in the United States." *Journal of Political Economy* 48 (April 1940): 222–37.

D. WAR AND DOMESTIC POLITICAL CONFLICT

Brooks, Robin. "Domestic Violence and America's Wars: A Historical Interpretation." In *Violence in America: Historical and Comparative Perspectives,* pp. 529–50. Ed. Hugh Davis Graham and Ted Robert Gurr. New York: Bantam Books, 1969.

Cantril, Hadley. "Opinion Trends in World War II: Some Guides to Interpretation." *Public Opinion Quarterly* 12 (Spring 1948): 30–44.

Flanigan, William H., and Fogelman, Edwin. "Patterns of Political Violence in Comparative Historical Perspective." *Comparative Politics* 3 (October 1970): 1–20.

Mathews, John M. "Political Parties and the War." *American Political Science Review* 13 (May 1919): 213–28.

Michels, Robert. "Party-Life in War-Time." In *Political Parties: A Sociological Study of the Oligarchical Tendencies of Modern Democracy,* pp. 357–63. Trans. Eden and Cedar Paul. New York: The Free Press, 1962.

Mueller, John E. "Trends in Popular Support for the Wars in Korea and Vietnam." *American Political Science Review* 65 (June 1971): 358-75.

———. *War, Presidents and Public Opinion.* New York: John Wiley and Sons, 1973.

Satow, Roberta. "Political Repression During Wartime: An Empirical Study of Simmel's Theory of Conflict." Ph.D. dissertation, New York University, 1972.

———. "The Dysfunctions of Social Conflict: Political Repression During Wartime." Brooklyn College, 1974.

Schaich, Warren. "A Relationship Between Collective Racial Violence and War." *Journal of Black Studies* 5 (June 1975): 374-94.

Stohl, Michael. "Linkages Between War and Domestic Political Violence in the United States, 1890-1923." In *Quasi-Experimental Approaches: Testing Theory and Evaluating Policy,* pp. 156-79. Ed. James A. Caporaso and Leslie L. Roos, Jr. Evanston, Ill.: Northwestern University Press, 1973.

———. "War and Domestic Political Violence in the United States 1890-1970: The American Capacity for Repression and Reaction." Ph.D. dissertation, Northwestern University, 1974.

———. "War and Domestic Political Violence: The Case of the United States 1890-1970." *Journal of Conflict Resolution* 19 (September 1975): 379-416.

———. *War and Domestic Political Violence: The American Capacity for Repression and Reaction.* Beverly Hills, Calif.: Sage Publications, 1976.

Tanter, Raymond. "International War and Domestic Turmoil: Some Contemporary Evidence." In *Violence in America: Historical and Comparative Perspectives,* pp. 550-69. Ed. Hugh Davis Graham and Ted Robert Gurr. New York: Bantam Books, 1969.

3. WAR AND CONCENTRATION

A. GOVERNMENTAL CONCENTRATION

Andic, Suphan, and Veverka, Jindrich. "The Growth of Government Expenditure in Germany since the Unification." *Finanzarchiv,* n.s., 23 (January 1964): 169-278.

Bator, Francis M. *The Question of Government Spending: Public Needs and Private Wants.* New York: Harper and Brothers, 1960.

Bean, Richard. "War and the Birth of the Nation State." *Journal of Economic History* 33 (March 1973): 203-21.

Bird, Richard M. "Wagner's 'Law' of Expanding State Activity." *Public Finance* 26 (1971): 1-26.

Carneiro, Robert L. "A Theory of the Origin of the State." *Science,* 21 August 1970, pp. 733-38.

Clayton, James L. "The Fiscal Limits of the Warfare-Welfare State: Defense and Welfare Spending in the United States since 1900." *Western Political Quarterly* 29 (September 1976): 364-83.

Crowley, Ronald W. "Long Swings in the Role of Government: An Analysis of Wars and Government Expenditures in Western Europe Since the Eleventh Century." *Public Finance* 26 (1971): 27-43.

Davies, David G. "The Concentration Process and the Growing Importance of Non-central Governments in Federal States." *Public Policy* 18 (Fall 1970): 649–57.

Fabricant, Solomon. *The Rising Trend of Government Employment.* New York: National Bureau of Economic Research, 1949.

Gupta Shibshankar P. "Public Expenditure and Economic Growth—A Time-Series Analysis." *Public Finance* 22 (1967): 423–61.

Kendrick, M. Slade. *A Century and a Half of Federal Expenditures.* New York: National Bureau of Economic Research, 1955.

Krane, Dale. "Longitudinal Patterns of Centralization and Development: Testing Theories of Government Organization." *Journal of Developing Areas* 12 (April 1978): 297–314.

Lane, Frederic C. "Economic Consequences of Organized Violence." *Journal of Economic History* 18 (December 1958): 401–17.

Lerner, Max. "The State in War Time." In *War in the Twentieth Century,* pp. 409–28. Ed. Willard Waller. New York: Random House, 1940.

McMahon, Walter W. "Cyclical Growth of Public Expenditure." *Public Finance* 26 (1971): 75–105.

Marr, William L. "The Expanding Role of Government and Wars: A Further Elaboration." *Public Finance* 29 (1974): 416–21.

Mosher, Frederick C., and Poland, Orville F. *The Costs of American Governments: Facts, Trends, Myths.* New York: Dodd, Mead and Company, 1964.

Musgrave, R. A., and Culbertson, J. M. "The Growth of Public Expenditures in the United States, 1890–1948." *National Tax Journal* 6 (June 1953): 97–115.

Peacock, Alan T., and Wiseman, Jack. *The Growth of Public Expenditure in the United Kingdom.* Princeton, N.J.: Princeton University Press, 1961.

Pryor, Frederic L. *Public Expenditures in Communist and Capitalist Nations.* Homewood, Ill.: Richard D. Irwin, Inc., 1968.

Rothwell, Charles Easton. "War and Economic Institutions." In *War as a Social Institution: The Historian's Perspective,* pp. 197–211. Ed. Jesse D. Clarkson and Thomas C. Cochran. New York: Columbia University Press, 1941.

Tussing, A. Dale, and Henning, John A. "Long-Run Growth of Nondefense Government Expenditures in the United States." *Public Finance Quarterly* 2 (April 1974): 202–22.

Veverka, J. "The Growth of Government Expenditure in the United Kingdom Since 1790." *Scottish Journal of Political Economy* 10 (February 1963): 111–27.

B. POPULATION CONCENTRATION

Bogue, Donald J. "Changes in Population Distribution Since 1940." *American Journal of Sociology* 56 (July 1950): 43–57.

Eskin, Leonard. "Sources of Wartime Labor Supply." *Monthly Labor Review* 59 (August 1944): 264–78.

Gibbs, Jack P. "Measures of Urbanization." *Social Forces* 45 (December 1966): 170–77.

———. "Further Observations on 'Measures of Urbanization.'" *Social Forces* 46 (March 1968): 400–405.

Goldfield, Edwin D. "The Wartime Labor Force in Major Industrial Areas." *Review of Economic Statistics* 27 (August 1945): 133-40.

Heberle, Rudolf. *The Impact of War on Population Redistribution in the South.* Papers of the Institute of Research and Training in the Social Sciences, no. 7. Nashville, Tenn.: Vanderbilt University Press, 1945.

Jones, F. Lancaster. "A Note on 'Measures of Urbanization,' With a Further Proposal." *Social Forces* 46 (December 1967): 275-79.

Lamb, Robert K. "Mobilization of Human Resources." *American Journal of Sociology* 58 (November 1942): 323-30.

Shryock, Henry S., Jr. "Internal Migration and the War." *Journal of the American Statistical Association* 38 (March 1943): 16-30.

_____. "Redistribution of Population: 1940 to 1950." *Journal of the American Statistical Association* 46 (December 1951): 417-37.

_____, and Eldridge, Hope Tisdale. "Internal Migration in Peace and War." *American Sociological Review* 12 (February 1947): 27-39.

Shryock, Henry S., Jr., and Larmon, Elizabeth A. "Some Longitudinal Data on Internal Migration." *Demography* 2 (1965): 579-92.

Taeuber, Conrad. "Wartime Population Changes in the United States." *Milbank Memorial Fund Quarterly* 24 (July 1946): 235-50.

C. INDUSTRIAL CONCENTRATION

Adelman, M. A. "The Measurement of Industrial Concentration." *Review of Economics and Statistics* 33 (November 1951): 269-96.

_____. "Monopoly and Concentration: Comparisons in Time and Space." In *Essays in Honour of Marco Fanno*, vol. 2: *Investigations in Economic Theory and Methodology*, pp. 1-24. Ed. Tullio Bagiotti. Padova: Edizioni Cedam, 1966.

_____. "Changes in Industrial Concentration." In *Monopoly Power and Economic Performance: The Problem of Industrial Concentration*, pp. 83-88. 3rd ed. Ed. Edwin Mansfield. New York: W. W. Norton and Company, 1974.

Bain, Joe S. "Economies of Scale." In *International Encyclopedia of the Social Sciences*, vol. 4, pp. 491-95. Ed. David L. Sills. New York: Macmillan and The Free Press, 1968.

Blair, John M. " 'The Measurement of Industrial Concentration': A Reply." *Review of Economics and Statistics* 34 (November 1952): 343-55.

_____. "On the Causes of Concentration." In *Die Konzentration in Der Wirtschaft*, vol. 2: *Ursachen der Konzentration*, pp. 815-37. Ed. Helmut Arndt. Berlin: Verlag von Duncker & Humblot, 1960.

_____. *Economic Concentration: Structure, Behavior and Public Policy.* Foreward by Gardiner C. Means. New York: Harcourt, Brace, Jovanovich, 1972.

Blaisdell, Thomas C., Jr. "Industrial Concentration in the War." *American Economic Review* 33 (March 1943): 159-61.

Burns, Arthur Robert. "Concentration of Production." *Harvard Business Review* 21 (Spring 1943): 277-90.

Collins, Norman R., and Preston, Lee E. "The Size Structure of the Largest Industrial Firms, 1909-1958." *American Economic Review* 51 (December 1961): 986-1011.

The Conference Board. *Anthology of Studies of Industrial Concentration by The Conference Board: 1958–1972.* New York: The Conference Board, March 1973.

Edwards, Corwin D., Stocking, George W., George, Edwin B., Berle, A. A., Jr., and Adelman, M. A. "Four Comments on 'The Measurement of Industrial Concentration': With a Rejoinder by Professor Adelman." *Review of Economics and Statistics* 34 (May 1952): 156–78.

Kaplan, A. D. H. *Big Enterprise in a Competitive System.* Washington: The Brookings Institution, 1954.

Lynch, David. *The Concentration of Economic Power.* New York: Columbia University Press, 1946.

Mansfield, Edwin, ed. *Monopoly Power and Economic Performance: The Problem of Industrial Concentration.* 3rd ed. New York: W. W. Norton and Company, 1974.

Myers, Charles A. "Wartime Concentration of Production." *Journal of Political Economy* 51 (June 1943): 222–34.

4. WAR AND INEQUALITY

A. PARTICIPATION, EXTRACTION, SOCIAL WELFARE, AND STRATIFICATION

Abrahamson, Mark. "Functionalism and the Functional Theory of Stratification: An Empirical Assessment." *American Journal of Sociology* 78 (March 1973): 1236–46.

Ames, Edward, and Rapp, Richard T. "The Birth and Death of Taxes: A Hypothesis." *Journal of Economic History* 37 (March 1977): 161–78.

Anderson, Mary. "Women's Status in Industry in World War 2." In *Yearbook of American Labor,* vol. 1: *War Labor Policies,* pp. 414–21. Ed. Colston E. Warne, Warren B. Catlin, Dorothy W. Douglas, J. Raymond Walsh, and Constance Williams. New York: Philosophical Library, 1945.

Caputo, David A. "New Perspectives on the Public Policy Implications of Defense and Welfare Expenditures in Four Modern Democracies: 1950–1970." *Policy Sciences* 6 (December 1975): 423–46.

Dabelko, David, and McCormick, James M. "Opportunity Costs of Defense: Some Cross-National Evidence." *Journal of Peace Research* 14 (1977): 145–54.

Fried, Morton H. "Warfare, Military Organization, and the Evolution of Society." *Anthropologica* 3 (1961): 134–47.

Friedman, Milton. "Price, Income, and Monetary Changes in Three Wartime Periods." *American Economic Review* 42 (May 1952): 612–25.

Garnier, Maurice A., and Hazelrigg, Lawrence E. "Military Organization and Distributional Inequality: An Examination of Andreski's Thesis." Indiana University, Center for International Policy Studies and Department of Sociology, n.d.

Hamilton, Earl J. "The Role of War in Modern Inflation." *Journal of Economic History* 37 (March 1977): 13–19.

Hollenhorst, Jerry, and Ault, Gary. "An Alternative Answer to: Who Pays for Defense?" *American Political Science Review* 65 (September 1971): 760–63.

Kaufman, Joyce P. "The Social Consequences of War, Great Britain: A Case Study." Paper presented at the annual meeting of the International Studies Association, Toronto, February 1976.

Long, Clarence D. *The Labor Force in Wartime America. Our Economy in War.*
Occasional Paper 14. New York: National Bureau of Economic Research, 1944.
_____. *The Labor Force in War and Transition: Four Countries.* Occasional Paper 36.
New York: National Bureau of Economic Research, 1952.
Meyers, Frederic. "Notes on Changes in the Distribution of Manufacturing Wage
Earners by Straight-Time Hourly Earnings, 1941-48." *Review of Economics and
Statistics* 32 (November 1950): 352-55.
Nottingham, Elizabeth K. "Toward an Analysis of the Effects of Two World Wars on
the Role and Status of Middle-class Women in the English-speaking World."
American Sociological Review 12 (December 1947): 666-75.
Robinson, Marshall A. "Federal Debt Management: Civil War, World War I, and
World War II." *American Economic Review* 45 (May 1955): 388-401.
Russett, Bruce M. "Who Pays for Defense?" *American Political Science Review* 63
(June 1969): 412-26.
_____. *What Price Vigilance? The Burdens of National Defense.* New Haven, Conn.:
Yale University Press, 1970.
_____. "Some Decisions in the Regression Analysis of Time-Series Data." In
Mathematical Applications in Political Science V, pp. 29-50. Ed. James F. Herndon
and Joseph L. Bernd. Charlottesville: University Press of Virginia, 1971.
Sorokin, Pitrim A. "War and Post-war Changes in Social Stratification of the Euro-
American Population." *American Sociological Review* 10 (April 1945): 294-303.
Stinchcombe, Arthur L. "Some Empirical Consequences of the Davis-Moore Theory
of Stratification." *American Sociological Review* 28 (October 1963): 805-8.
Titmuss, Richard M. "War and Social Policy." In *Essays on 'The Welfare State,'* pp.
75-87. Boston: Beacon Press, 1969; originally published 1958.
Wilensky, Harold L. *The Welfare State and Equality: Structural and Ideological Roots
of Public Expenditures.* Berkeley and Los Angeles: University of California Press,
1975.

B. INCOME INEQUALITY

(1) Empirical

Adler, John H. "The Fiscal System, the Distribution of Income, and Public Welfare."
In *Fiscal Policies and the American Economy,* pp. 359-409. Ed. Kenyon E. Poole.
New York: Prentice-Hall, 1951.
Atkinson, Thomas R. "Some Frontiers of Size-Distribution Research." In *An Ap-
praisal of the 1950 Census Income Data,* pp. 29-38. National Bureau of Economic
Research, Conference on Research in Income and Wealth. Studies in Income and
Wealth, vol. 28. Princeton, N.J.: Princeton University Press, 1958.
Brady, Dorothy S. "Research on the Size Distribution of Income." *Studies in Income
and Wealth: Volume 13,* pp. 2-55. Conference on Research in Income and Wealth.
New York: National Bureau of Economic Research, 1951.
Budd, Edward C., and Seiders, David F. "The Impact of Inflation on the Distribution
of Income and Wealth." *American Economic Review* 61 (May 1971): 128-38.
Conrad, Alfred H. "Redistribution Through Government Budgets in the United States,
1950." In *Income Redistribution and Social Policy: A Set of Studies,* pp. 178-267.
Ed. Alan T. Peacock. London: Jonathan Cape, 1954.

Copeland, Morris A. "The Social and Economic Determinants of the Distribution of Income in the United States." *American Economic Review* 37 (March 1947): 56–75.

Denison, Edward F. "Income Types and the Size Distribution." *American Economic Review* 44 (May 1954): 254–69.

Garvy, George. "Inequality of Income: Causes and Measurement." In *Studies in Income and Wealth: Volume 15*, pp. 25–47. New York: National Bureau of Economic Research, 1952.

Gillespie, W. Irwin. "Effect of Public Expenditures on the Distribution of Income." In *Essays in Fiscal Federalism*, pp. 122–86. Ed. Richard A. Musgrave. Washington: The Brookings Institution, 1965.

Goldsmith, Selma F. "The Relation of Census Income Distribution Statistics to other Income Data." In *An Appraisal of the 1950 Census Income Data*, pp. 65–107. National Bureau of Economic Research, Conference on Research in Income and Wealth. Studies in Income and Wealth, vol. 23. Princeton, N.J.: Princeton University Press, 1958.

———. "Impact of the Income Tax on Socio-Economic Groups of Families in the United States." In *Income Redistribution and the Statistical Foundations of Economic Policy*, pp. 248–79. Income and Wealth: Series X. Ed. Colin Clark and Geer Stuvel. New Haven, Conn.: International Association for Research in Income and Wealth, 1964.

Hollister, Robinson G., and Palmer, John L. "The Impact of Inflation on the Poor." In *Redistribution to the Rich and the Poor: The Grants Economics of Income Distribution*, pp. 240–70. Ed. Kenneth E. Boulding and Martin Pfaff. Belmont, Calif.: Wadsworth Publishing Company, 1972.

Horowitz, Ann R. "The Pattern and Causes of Changes in White-Nonwhite Income Differences: 1947–1972." In *Patterns of Racial Discrimination*, vol. II: *Employment and Income*, pp. 149–66. Ed. George M. von Furstenberg, Ann R. Horowitz, and Bennett Harrison. Lexington, Mass.: D. C. Heath and Company, 1974.

Metcalf, Charles E. "The Size Distribution of Personal Income During the Business Cycle." *American Economic Review* 59 (September 1969): 657–68.

———. "Fiscal Policy and the Poor: The Case of Vietnam." *Public Policy* 18 (Winter 1970): 187–209.

———. *An Econometric Model of the Income Distribution*. Chicago: Markham Publishing, 1972.

Miller, Herman P. "Factors Related to Recent Changes in Income Distribution in the United States." *Review of Economics and Statistics* 33 (August 1951): 214–18.

Moore, Geoffrey H. "Secular Changes in the Distribution of Income." *American Economic Review* 42 (May 1952): 527–44.

Musgrave, R. A. "Estimating the Distribution of the Tax Burden." In *Income Redistribution and the Statistical Foundations of Economic Policy*, pp. 186–219. Income and Wealth: Series X. Ed. Colin Clark and Geer Stuvel. New Haven, Conn.: International Association for Research in Income and Wealth, 1964.

———, Case, Karl E., and Leonard, Herman. "The Distribution of Fiscal Burdens and Benefits." *Public Finance Quarterly* 2 (July 1974): 259–311.

Nordhaus, William D. "The Effects of Inflation on the Distribution of Economic Welfare." *Journal of Money, Credit, and Banking* 5 (February 1973): 465–504.

Okner, Benjamin A. "Transfer Payments: Their Distribution and Role in Reducing Poverty." In *Redistribution to the Rich and the Poor: The Grants Economics of Income Distribution*, pp. 62-77. Ed. Kenneth E. Boulding and Martin Pfaff. Belmont, Calif.: Wadsworth Publishing Company, 1972.

––––––. "Individual Taxes and the Distribution of Income." In *The Personal Distribution of Income and Wealth*, pp. 45-73. Studies in Income and Wealth, vol. 39. Ed. James D. Smith. New York: National Bureau of Economic Research, 1975.

Paukert, Felix. "Income Distribution at Different Levels of Development: A Survey of Evidence." *International Labour Review* 108 (August-September 1973): 97-125.

Pechman, Joseph A. "Distribution of Income Before and After Federal Income Taxes, 1941 and 1947." *Studies in Income and Wealth: Volume 13*, pp. 186-213. Conference on Research in Income and Wealth. New York: National Bureau of Economic Research, 1951.

Projector, Dorothy S., Weiss, Gertrude S., and Thoresen, Erling T. "Composition of Income as Shown by the Survey of Financial Characteristics of Consumers." In *Six Papers on the Distribution of Wealth and Income*, pp. 107-56. Ed. Lee Soltow. Studies in Income and Wealth, vol. 33. New York: National Bureau of Economic Research, 1969.

Roberti, Paolo. "Income Distribution: A Time-Series and a Cross-Section Study." *Economic Journal* 84 (September 1974): 629-38.

Schultz, T. Paul. "Secular Trends and Cyclical Behavior of Income Distribution in the United States: 1944-1965." In *Six Papers on the Size Distribution of Wealth and Income*, pp. 75-100. Ed. Lee Soltow. Studies in Income and Wealth, vol. 33. New York: National Bureau of Economic Research, 1969.

Smelker, Mary W. "Shifts in the Concentration of Income." *Review of Economics and Statistics* 30 (August 1948): 215-22.

Soltow, Lee. "Shifts in Factor Payments and Income Distribution." *American Economic Review* 49 (June 1959): 395-98.

––––––. "The Share of Lower Income Groups in Income." *Review of Economics and Statistics* 47 (November 1965): 429-33.

Stauffacher, Charles. "The Effects of Government Expenditures and Tax Withdrawals upon Income Distribution, 1930-1939." In *Public Policy*, pp. 232-61. Ed. C. J. Friedrich and Edward S. Mason. Cambridge, Mass.: Harvard University, Graduate School of Public Administration, 1941.

Thurow, Lester C. "Analyzing the American Income Distribution." *American Economic Review* 60 (May 1970): 261-69.

Tucker, Rufus S. "The Distribution of Government Burdens and Benefits." *American Economic Review* 43 (May 1953): 518-34.

Tuckman, Howard P., and Brosch, Gary. "Changes in Personal Income and Their Effect on Income Shares." *Southern Economic Journal* 41 (July 1974): 78-86.

U.S. Congress. Joint Economic Committee. *The American Distribution of Income: A Structural Problem*, by Lester C. Thurow and Robert E. B. Lucas. Washington: Government Printing Office, 17 March 1972.

Vroman, Wayne. "Changes in Black Workers' Relative Earnings: Evidence from the 1960s." In *Patterns of Racial Discrimination*, vol. II: *Employment and Income*, pp. 167-87. Ed. George M. von Furstenberg, Ann R. Horowitz, and Bennett Harrison. Lexington, Mass.: D. C. Heath and Company, 1974.

(2) United States

Brady, Dorothy S. "Measurement and Interpretation of the Income Distribution in the United States." In *Income and Wealth: Series VI*, pp. 78–97. International Association for Research in Income and Wealth. Ed. Milton Gilbert and Richard Stone. London: Bowes and Bowes, 1957.

Budd, Edward C. "Postwar Changes in the Size Distribution of Income in the U.S." *American Economic Review* 60 (May 1970): 247–60.

Burkhead, Jesse. "Vietnam and the Great Income Reshuffle." *Challenge* 15 (May-June 1967): 12–13, 35–37.

Farley, Reynolds. "Trends in Racial Inequalities: Have the Gains of the 1960s Disappeared in the 1970s?" *American Sociological Review* 42 (April 1977): 189–208.

Gastwirth, Joseph L. "The Estimation of the Lorenz Curve and Gini Index." *Review of Economics and Statistics* 54 (August 1972): 306–16.

Goldsmith, Selma F. "Statistical Information on the Distribution of Income by Size in the United States." *American Economic Review* 40 (May 1950): 321–41.

————. "Appraisal of Basic Data Available for Constructing Income Size Distributions." In *Studies in Income and Wealth: Volume 13*, pp. 266–373. Conference on Research in Income and Wealth. New York: National Bureau of Economic Research, 1951.

————. "Changes in the Size Distribution of Income." *American Economic Review* 47 (May 1957): 504–18.

————, Jaszi, George, Kaitz, Hyman, and Liebenberg, Maurice. "Size Distribution of Income Since the Mid-Thirties." *Review of Economics and Statistics* 36 (February 1954): 1–32.

Haley, Bernard F. "Changes in the Distribution of Income in the United States." In *The Distribution of National Income*, pp. 3–40. Ed. Jean Marchal and Bernard Ducros. New York: St. Martin's Press, 1968.

Horowitz, Ann R. "Trends in the Distribution of Family Income within and between Racial Groups." In *Patterns of Racial Discrimination*, vol. II: *Employment and Income*, pp. 197–211. Ed. George M. von Furstenberg, Ann R. Horowitz, and Bennett Harrison. Lexington, Mass.: D. C. Heath and Company, 1974.

Johnson, Norris O. "The Pareto Law." *Review of Economic Statistics* 19 (February 1937): 20–26.

Kuznets, Simon. *Shares of Upper Income Groups in Income and Savings*. New York: National Bureau of Economic Research, 1953.

Lampman, Robert J. "Recent Changes in Income Inequality Reconsidered." *American Economic Review* 44 (June 1954): 251–68.

Lebergott, Stanley. *The American Economy: Income, Wealth, and Want*. Princeton, N.J.: Princeton University Press, 1976.

Menderhausen, Horst. *Changes in Income Distribution During the Great Depression*. Studies in Income and Wealth: Volume 7. Conference on Research in Income and Wealth. New York: National Bureau of Economic Research, 1946.

Merwin, C. L., Jr. "American Studies of the Distribution of Wealth and Income by Size." In *Studies in Income and Wealth: Volume 3*, pp. 3–84. Conference on Research in National Income and Wealth. New York: National Bureau of Economic Research, 1939.

Miller, S. M., and Roby, Pamela A. *The Future of Inequality.* New York: Basic Books, 1970.

Morgan, James N., David, Martin H., Cohen, Wilbur J., and Brazer, Harvey E. *Income and Welfare in the United States.* A Study by the Survey Research Center, Institute for Social Research, University of Michigan. New York: McGraw-Hill Book Company, 1962.

Schnitzer, Martin. *Income Distribution: A Comparative Study of the United States, Sweden, West Germany, East Germany, the United Kingdom, and Japan.* New York: Praeger Publishers, 1974.

Schultz, T. Paul. *Long Term Change in Personal Income Distribution: Theoretical Approaches, Evidence and Explanations.* Santa Monica, Calif.: Rand Corporation, P-4767, January 1972.

Solow, Robert M. "Income Inequality Since the War." In *Postwar Economic Trends in the United States,* pp. 91-138. Ed. Ralph E. Freeman. New York: Harper and Brothers, 1960.

Soltow, Lee C. "Evidence on Income Inequality in the United States, 1866-1965." *Journal of Economic History* 29 (June 1969): 279-86.

Swanson, Helen. "A Guide to Income Distributions." *The Conference Board Business Record* 17 (July 1960): 48-51.

Thurow, Lester C. *Generating Inequality: Mechanisms of Distribution in the U.S. Economy.* New York: Basic Books, 1975.

Tucker, Rufus S. "The Distribution of Income among Income Taxpayers in the United States, 1863-1935." *Quarterly Journal of Economics* 52 (August 1938): 547-87.

Turner, Jonathan H., and Starnes, Charles E. *Inequality: Privilege & Poverty in America.* Pacific Palisades, Calif.: Goodyear Publishing, 1976.

U.S. Bureau of the Census. *Income Distribution in the United States,* by Herman P. Miller. A 1960 Census Monograph, 1966.

U.S. Congress. Joint Economic Committee. Subcommittee on Economic Statistics. *The Distribution of Personal Income: A Study of Statistics on the Size Distribution of Personal Income in the United States,* by T. Paul Schultz. Joint Committee Print, 88th Cong., December 1964.

————. Temporary National Economic Committee. *Investigation of Concentration of Economic Power,* monograph no. 4: *Concentration and Composition of Individual Incomes, 1918-1937,* by Adolph J. Goldenthal. Senate Committee Print, 1940.

U.S. Department of Commerce. Bureau of the Census. *Income Distribution in the United States,* by Herman P. Miller. Washington: Government Printing Office, 1966.

5. WAR ECONOMICS

American Economic Mobilization: A Study in the Mechanism of War. Cambridge, Mass.: Harvard Law Review Association, 1942.

Brown University Economists. *Introduction to War Economics.* Ed. Alfred C. Neal. Chicago: Richard D. Irwin, 1942.

Burnham, John. *Total War: The Economic Theory of a War Economy.* Boston: Meador Publishing, 1943.

Chandler, Lester V., and Wallace, Donald H., eds. *Economic Mobilization and Stabilization: Selected Materials on the Economics of War and Defense.* New York: Henry Holt and Company, 1951.

Clark, J. Maurice, Hamilton, Walton H., and Moulton, Harold G., eds. *Readings in the Economics of War.* Chicago: University of Chicago Press, 1918.

Cole, G. D. H. "Mobilization and Demobilization." In *Encyclopaedia of the Social Sciences,* vol. 10, pp. 555–64. Ed. Edwin R. A. Seligman. New York: Macmillan, 1934.

Colm, Gerhard. "War Finance." In *Encyclopaedia of the Social Sciences,* vol. 15, pp. 347–52. Ed. Edwin R. A. Seligman. New York: Macmillan, 1934.

Condliffe, J. B. "War and Economics: A Review Article." *Journal of Political Economy* 51 (April 1943): 157–65.

Filipetti, G. *Industrial Production in Time of War.* St. Louis: John S. Swift Company, 1943.

International Labour Office. *Studies in War Economics.* Series B (Economic Conditions), no. 33. Montreal: International Labour Office, 1941.

Jack, D. T. *Studies in Economic Warfare.* New York: Chemical Publishing, 1941.

Johnson, Alvin. "War Economics." In *Encyclopaedia of the Social Sciences,* vol. 15, pp. 342–47. Ed. Edwin R. A. Seligman. New York: Macmillan, 1934.

Lincoln, George A. *Economics of National Security.* 2nd ed. New York: Prentice-Hall, 1954.

Menderhausen, Horst. *The Economics of War.* Rev. ed. New York: Prentice-Hall, 1943.

Neurath, Otto. "The Theory of War Economy as a Separate Discipline." In *Empiricism and Sociology,* pp. 125–30. Ed. Marie Neurath and Robert S. Cohen. Boston: D. Reidel Publishing, 1973.

Oxford University, Institute of Statistics. *Studies in War Economics.* Oxford: Basil Blackwell, 1947.

Rosenbaum, E. M. "War Economics: A Bibliographical Approach." *Economica* 9 (February 1942): 64–94.

Schumpeter, Joseph A. "The Crisis of the Tax State." Trans. W. F. Stolper and R. A. Musgrave. In *International Economic Papers, No. 4: Translations Prepared for the International Economic Association,* pp. 5–38. Ed. Alan T. Peacock, Wolfgang F. Stolper, Ralph Turvey, and Elizabeth Henderson. New York: Macmillan, 1954.

Severson, Lewis. "Some Current Books on the Economics of Total War." *Journal of Political Economy* 51 (April 1943): 169–73.

Shaw, Edward S., and Tarshis, Lorie. "A Program for Economic Mobilization." *American Economic Review* 41 (March 1951): 30–50.

Silberner, Edmund. *The Problem of War in Nineteenth Century Economic Thought.* Trans. Alexander H. Krappe. Princeton, N.J.: Princeton University Press, 1946.

Spiegel, Henry William. *The Economics of Total War.* The Century Studies in Economics Series. New York: D. Appleton-Century Company, 1942.

Stein, Emanuel, and Backman, Jules, eds. *War Economics.* New York: Farrar and Rinehart, 1942.

Steiner, George A., ed. *Economic Problems of War.* New York: John Wiley and Sons, 1942.

Stern, Walter M. "Wehrwirtschaft: A German Contribution to Economics." *Economic History Review,* 2nd ser., 13 (December 1960): 270–81.

Tobin, Harold J., and Bidwell, Percy W. *Mobilizing Civilian America.* New York: Council on Foreign Relations, 1940.

Wolf, Franz B. "Economy in War Time." In *War in the Twentieth Century,* pp. 363–408. Ed. Willard Waller. New York: Random House, 1940.

Wright, Chester W., ed. *Economic Problems of War and Its Aftermath.* Chicago: University of Chicago Press, 1942.

6. METHODOLOGY

Campbell, Donald T. "From Description to Experimentation: Interpreting Trends as Quasi-Experiments." In *Problems in Measuring Change,* pp. 212–42. Ed. Chester W. Harris. Madison: University of Wisconsin Press, 1963.

_____. "Reforms as Experiments." *American Psychologist* 24 (April 1969): 409–29.

_____. "Definitional versus Multiple Operationalism." *et al.* 2 (Summer 1969): 14–17.

_____, and Stanley, Julian C. *Experimental and Quasi-Experimental Designs for Research.* Chicago: Rand McNally, 1963.

Caporaso, James A., and Roos, Leslie L., Jr., eds. *Quasi-Experimental Approaches: Testing Theory and Evaluating Policy.* Evanston, Ill.: Northwestern University Press, 1973.

Glass, Gene V., Willson, Victor L., and Gottman, John M. *Design and Analysis of Time-Series Experiments.* Boulder: Colorado Associated University Press, 1975.

Hibbs, Douglas A., Jr. "Problems of Statistical Estimation and Causal Inference in Time-Series Regression Models." In *Sociological Methodology 1973–1974,* pp. 252–308. Ed. Herbert L. Costner. San Francisco: Jossey-Bass Publishers, 1974.

_____. "On Analyzing the Effects of Policy Interventions: Box-Jenkins and Box-Tiao vs. Structural Equation Models." In *Sociological Methodology 1977,* pp. 137–79. Ed. David R. Heise. San Francisco: Jossey-Bass Publishers, 1977.

Nelson, Charles R. *Applied Time Series Analysis for Managerial Forecasting.* San Francisco: Holden-Day, 1973.

Riecken, Henry W., and Boruch, Robert F., eds. *Social Experimentation: A Method for Planning and Evaluating Social Intervention.* New York: Academic Press, 1974.

INDEX

143

THE JOHNS HOPKINS UNIVERSITY PRESS

This book was composed in VIP Times Roman text and
Melior Bold display type by The Composing Room of
Michigan. It was printed and bound by Universal
Lithographers, Inc.